Fly Fishing in Maine

Photo by Paul Knaut, Jr.

Al Raychard's

Fly Fishing in Maine

The Complete Guide to the Best Fly Fishing in Maine.

THE THORNDIKE PRESS

THORNDIKE, MAINE

Library of Congress Cataloging in Publication Data

Raychard, Al.
  Al Raychard's Fly fishing in Maine.

  1. Fishing—Maine—Guide-books.
  2. Fly fishing.
I. Title. II. Title: Fly fishing in Maine.
SH503.R39   799.1'2'09741   80-12126
ISBN 0-89621-056-1
ISBN 0-89621-005-3 (pbk.)

DEDICATED...

to my wife, Sandra, who, like no one else, has been with me all the way.

ACKNOWLEDGEMENTS

The compilation of a guide book such as this one is, in many ways, a trying task. But with the challenges and frustration from beginning to end, there are rewards as well—notably, the opportunity to meet fellow fly fishermen. And, indeed, the accuracy of this publication could not have been offered without interest and imput from many individuals—fishermen and friends scattered throughout this magnificent state of Maine. In actuality, Chapter Six, WHERE TO GO, is as much their work as it is mine. And it is to the following that Chapter Six is dedicated and many thanks were given:

To Ed Webb of The Forks, for his data on the ponds in Somerset County and for his friendship down through the years; to Roger Lane, owner of Gray Ghost Camps on Moosehead Lake, for his helpful information; to Bob Paradis, friend and owner of Flybuck Camps in Rangeley; to Ken Sassi of Weatherby's in Grand Lake Stream for his information on that famed retreat; to Phil Foster; and particular thanks to Stan Milton of Lakewood Lodge on the Rapid River; and to Mr. Fred Martineau of Rumford, with whom I have spent many cherished hours fishing that favorite salmon haven.

Al Raychard
Saco, Maine
February 4, 1980

Photo by Paul Knaut, Jr.

TABLE OF CONTENTS

Penobscot County, In Piscataquis County. In Somerset County. In Washington County. In York County. In other counties. In Baxter State Park. Maps of the "Top Ten". A word on saltwater brown trout.

Flying In: "Wilderness". How to plan a trip—and when. What to take with you. Sources of fly-in information. **Hiking In**: It's worth the trouble! What to take with you. Sources of hiking information. Some good hike-in ponds: Along the Appalachian Trail. Within Baxter State Park. Near Mt. Blue State Park.

Salmo salar takes a fly. The fish—what, where, and when. Atlantic salmon gear. Technique. **The Rivers**: The Penobscot. The Narraguagus. The Machias and East Machias. The Dennys. The Sheepscot. The Pleasant. The Union. Other salmon rivers. Summary chart.

Rods. Reels. Lines. Leaders. Vests. Waders. Landing nets. Fly boxes. Fly dressing. Sun glasses. Where to get it.

Sources of information.

INTRODUCTION

In my mind I have an image of Maine, and at its center is a clearly defined, mind's-eye view of a lake surrounded by spruces. The surface of the lake is a mirror, and on it floats a canoe, and in the canoe sits a fly fisherman casting to the lake surface, where myriad dimples suggest the opening sprinkles of a rain shower. He is fishing to rising trout, of course, doing important things by himself. This, to me, is Maine. It is an image that received its first gentle shapings in my youth, and it has added new trappings as the years passed and my experiences gathered in number and meaning. In truth, I see myself in that canoe, as do all fly fisherman.

I don't *know* Maine. Only those who live in its backwoods truly know this green-carpeted state where lakes and streams—glimpsed from above— sparkle in the sun. But I know Maine the way one can know a rainbow or the swarm of a mayfly hatch on a sunny May morning when the air is full of sweet pollen and the sun lights the new leaves and turns the world green. Maine is one of those places where all of nature has conspired and created a special physical numenon . . . natural magic where you expect to find fays and elves.

And it is more than that. This special place has created a gritty citizenry, especially the Maine woods people, the ones who have heard the winds sough high in the hardwood ridges, sigh in the great spruce swamps and whistle across the lakes—the ones who decided not to depart for the lure and lucre of city life.

During the past three centuries this society of woods people became a culture that depended on natural harvests to survive. I've had a love affair with that kind of culture since I was old enough to hunt and fish and read. The love affair was truly my creation: I admire the character of people who survive in unforgiving surroundings where life is wrung from the ground and appor- tioned carefully among deserving neighbors. I admire the esthetics of frugality that produce tools which feel good in the hand, artifacts fashioned from native materials, and I admire people with strong character. Of course, Maine woods people did the same things with materials that other peoples of the world have done. But there is a rare stamp on Maine things, and on Maine people.

For me, the most telling evidence of a special cultural legacy are the flies tied by Maine fishermen. For those unfamiliar with fly-fishing my singling out flies with names that sing, like Parmachene Belle, or tell stories, like the Warden's Worry, as symbols of cultural distinction may seem puzzling. But fly fishermen will understand that the woodsmen of Maine loved their fishing above all other things life could offer. It should not surprise fly fishermen, then, to learn that pioneering feats in fly-fishing methods and fly-tying techniques happened in the Maine woods. There were waters that over the decades became famous far beyond the borders of Maine for a particular species of fish (often the brook trout), a killing fly pattern or in some cases for a man who lived and fished effectively, and with that certain grace that sets some men apart.

A long way to go, perhaps, to thank Al Raychard for reminding us of what is best in Maine. A long way to go to explain why this little book—which tells a mouthfull on where-to, when-to and how-to along with the who-did-what—is valuable.

Maine is a friendly place, particularly for fly fishermen. And I'm sure it can take without harm this gentle flattery that we reserve for places and people we admire.

—John Randolph

Chapter 1
FISHERMAN'S ETHICS

It had been a long drive to the campground at South Arm on Lower Richardson Lake. My wife, Sandra, and I had left our southern Maine home early that June morning, wanting to arrive at the lake before daylight. We quickly unpacked the pickup, leaving the campsite in a wickedly devastated state, and launched the boat and started the five-mile journey to the Rapid River at Middle Dam, one of our favorite fly fishing retreats.

A thin, ghostly fog hung over the water that morning. As we docked at the large log pilings near Middle Dam and mated rods with reels, the sun cleared the mountaintops like a golden eye. But its beauty had been matched by a more capturing sound—the roar of water as it flushed past the dam gates, emptied into Dam Pool, and left again in a torrent of whitewater into Harbec Pool and beyond. Already, that anxious feeling stirred within me, and with intensifing impatience we walked down the steep bank to the river.

Only one other fly fisherman was visible. He was stationed on a small rocky point at the lower end of the pool, diligently trying to work a dry fly close to a possible salmon lie far out of his casting reach. As I expected, the offering landed far short of its proper mark and was quickly whirled away by the current. He was clearly unfamiliar with the river, perhaps with landlocked

13

salmon fishing in general, for several fine lies were visible only yards from his casting point.

"Where do you want to try?" I asked my companion.

"I don't know—I think I'll try off the dam in those eddys. How about you?"

"I think I'll just watch for a few minutes; we've got plenty of time. I think I'll have a smoke and just watch. Remember—don't overcast, and allow plenty of drift."

"I know, I know. *You* just remember to remember; we'll see what the tally is when we're done!"

The downstream angler conducted another tragic upstream cast with no luck. As I brought a match to my pipe, a salmon rolled to his left—I wondered if he had caught the rise. He hadn't. After several more unsuccessful attempts to reach that "all-important lie", he stripped in his line and began to change flies. My turn, I thought.

Another salmon kissed the surface slightly downstream, but he was of little interest to me. The "grand-dads', I knew, would be in the faster water, where temperatures were more suitable and cover more to their liking.

I had learned my lesson a year earlier about salmon on the Rapid, particularly in Middle Dam Pool. They hold in lies extremely close to shore—at times you fish with more leader than line. With this thought in mind, I stripped off twenty feet of line and presented my fly slightly upstream past a submerged rock. The grasshopper pattern drifted past its mark and, after several mends of the line, reached its zenith downstream—untouched.

The fly was quickly placed on its mark once again with a single sweep. But this time, as it passed the rock on a swirling current, a salmon rose to the surface and, with a violent downward plunge, accepted it. I gently lifted the rod tip and the line came taut.

By the resistance on the end of the leader, I knew the fish was not one of the lunkers I was stalking. But his characteristic belligerence, aided by the current, still made the battle both impressive and thrilling. Keeping a steady strain on the line lessened the strength of my adversary, and he slowly came to the net—the fish reached fifteen inches, but was in fine condition, a trait of Rapid River landlocked salmon.

The hook was impaled in the maxillary area (upper jaw). Without taking the fish from the water, I carefully worked the barb loose, held the specimen freely under the belly until equilibrium was restored, and watched as he returned to the river. I was rewarded in the knowledge that I had won, and that he would be there for another day.

The fisherman I had been observing earlier had moved closer to me now. He had watched my antics with unusual curiosity, but had said nothing. His efforts, I noticed, were still going unrewarded, but it was his look of disbelief when I released the fish which stuck in my mind as I returned to the river for another try.

A good fifteen minutes elasped with no action on my line. Sandra caught and released one fish after my escapade, but other than that the river was quiet. The sun had cleared the treetops, and I figured the brightness was keeping the fish secluded. Reluctantly, I made a long cast, quartering upstream to a shadowed riffle next to the dam. With the current strong, and with so much line in the water, I knew the drag would allow only a short drift, but only a short time was needed. A salmon immediately accepted the offering and started on a rampage with the current.

The arc of the rod and power on the end of the line this time indicated that a fair-sized fish had fallen victim to my artificial. The current could be deceiving, but the way the fish moved freely against the current as well as with it seemed to point to some power on the hook. A succession of rolls, and a magnificent midstream clearing of the water, confirmed my suspicions of his size—I knew the battle had only begun. The salmon continued to fight belligerently, powerfully, with aerobatic skills characteristic of his breed. Hoping to maneuver him into the current, I lifted the rod higher and slowly moved downstream, praying that he would move into a full flow area and tire. The fish seemed to read my mind, however, and my tactic went unrewarded.

A downstream run with the current, taking an extra twenty yards of line, was followed by another series of rolls and clearing leaps. *Such resistance*, I thought. *He can't last much longer.* And indeed, the salmon's reluctance to be controlled by a foreign power began to subside. The power in the rod transformed through the line was taking its toll, and finally, the fish came within view. As expected, the sight of the net prompted a final surge for freedom, but his strength was gone. Minutes later, the fish rested in the net.

The salmon, a male, reached slightly over nineteen inches according to my scale, the largest specimen I had ever taken on the Rapid. As I worked to free the hook, the downstream fisherman appeared. "That's some fish—a male, huh?" I confirmed that it was and gently rested the exhausted "salar" in my hands as Sandra started to take pictures. Half a roll of film later, I waded in knee-deep and started to undulate the fish in the water, head facing upstream. His strength quickly returned, and he lifted from my hands on his own and disappeared into the current.

Again, that look of disbelief on the fisherman's face was the first thing that hit me. "Do you always do that?" he asked.

"Most of the time. I'd rather catch 'em than eat 'em, wouldn't you?"

For the first time in my travels, I came across a fisherman who really didn't know what to say. He exclaimed something about liking the taste of salmon, said he couldn't get enough of them, and that he had enough trouble catching them without releasing some. As Sandra and I gathered up our gear and started up the hill to the boat, we wished him good luck. But under my breath I muttered, "Thank God." I do hope he heard me.

For too long, the angling fraternity has held the belief that, to be good fishermen, we must kill the fish we catch—that an empty creel proves nothing, while a half-dozen dead trout or salmon proves all. This belief has been bred into us by our fathers and grandfathers, and will be a most difficult syndrome to break. But break it we must if appreciable wild trout and salmon resources are to be with us by the year 2000.

Never before has the need for more drastic catch-and-release and conservation practices been so evident. Our trout and salmon fisheries, although better in specific areas than they were a decade ago, are generally on a downward plunge. Destruction and pollution of habitat, acid rain, over-fishing, and the opening of once-inaccessible country, particularly here in Maine, are all contributing to these species' decline—and additional environmental threats are being added each day.

Because of their fragile characteristics, these fish are rapidly losing the battle for survival. And they will eventually lose the war as well, unless measures are taken to curtail adverse factors.

The fly fisherman is a special breed of sportsman—and I like to think that there is deep love and respect for our cold water species in the hearts of all who enjoy the art. The way we handle ourselves along the stream, however, and the etiquette we follow, paint a clear picture of our personal concern and respect not only for our cherished quarry, but for the reputation of the art itself and of our fellow anglers. It is, indeed, each fisherman's admiration for, and understanding of, his adversary which could greatly assist in the war for survival and continue to make true fly fishermen the envy of the angling world. It is the streamside job of each of us who do understand and appreciate the importance of catch-and-release practices to assist those who do not yet understand. And to explain to them that competition should not prevail between anglers, but between man and this truly unique and intelligent water-bound creation.

The belief that "dead fish prove an angler's ability and skill" is a good starting point from which to build our argument. We must get across the point that the true challenge to all fishermen is to successfully entice a trout or salmon to the hook with an artificial lure and play him skillfully to the net—and, most importantly, to release our opponent after he has given his best; that the reward for our efforts comes from the knowledge that we won the contest, but that the fish will be there tomorrow for another round. It is

Fishing in Baxter State Park

understandable to kill a specimen on occasion, if a desire for their taste is suggested. But it is completely ludicrous to kill these fish for the sake of proving one's ability, or to store them in the freezer simply to save money at the grocery store.

Better communications among fishermen will lead to better ethics by all. As fishermen who appreciate our resources, and who practice catch-and-release, we should not hesitate to assist those beginners in the art—from the selection of proper flies down to their presentation. Share your knowledge and experience—it is proof of your dedication to preserving the resource, and is the mark of a knowledgeable angler.

On the stream, it is an unwritten rule that a riffle area or pool already occupied is off limits unless permission is obtained to enter. And, if permission is given, allow a wide berth out of respect for the other angler. When a fish is hooked by a fellow fisherman, we should reel in and allow plenty of free area for the confrontation; an angler with hooked fish should have an undisputed right-of-way. And above all, we should remember to be gentlemen (or ladies), and considerate toward fellow casters and our quarry—this is one of the prime qualities which marks true fly fishermen.

For most of us, catching a wild trout or salmon is truly a challenge—but releasing him properly is equally as important if that fish is to live for another day. Releasing brook trout from a canoe is often easier than liberating landlocked salmon in a river or stream, but in all cases, the fish should ideally be left in the water while the hook is being removed. If it is absolutely necessary to land the fish, it should be for as short a time as possible, and our hands should be wet before handling them.

Fish too large or powerful for the net, such as Atlantic salmon and some landlocked salmon and brown trout, should be gripped firmly around the tail (in the caudal peduncle area) and brought to shore, where the hook can then be worked free. If it is necessary to grab the fish other than by the tail, do so firmly but gently around the back of the head over the gill covers; never squeeze a trout or salmon around the belly. Longnose pliers make excellent hook removers and allow minimum human contact with the fish.

Smaller fish, such as brook trout and the majority of landlocked salmon and browns, which can be netted, should be left in the net while the fly is being removed. Again, grasp the specimen firmly around the back of the head with wet hands; do not lift a fish by the gills if it is to be released. Most smaller fish hooked behind the maxillary bone can easily be released without taking them from the water. If the hook is imbedded into the upper or lower jaw, however, extreme care should be taken. If the hook cannot be worked free, the leader should be cut as close to the hook's eye as possible.

Once the hook has been removed, our responsibility of liberating the fish is only half done. The battle between a cold water salmonid and an angler is an excruciating struggle which drains all the strength and metabolic senses the fish possesses.

A fish will come to the net, or rather can be maneuvered into a net, only after his power of resistance has been completely exhausted, unless he is too small to fight the power of the rod from the start. When we release our adversary, therefore, it is highly important to offer some assistance to help him regain the strength we have taken and, during battle, enjoyed. This is easily done—gently hold the fish in open hands with head pointed into the current, or upstream. Such a refuge offers the spent fish precious minutes to regain the strength and oxgyen lost during his struggle for freedom. Severely exhausted trout, and salmon as well, will lie gently in your hands for several moments, undulating their tails and gill covers, then drift slowly off into their habitat once strength and the required senses have been restored. This is truly a pleasing and rewarding chapter of our art, one which is as memorable to me as the battle itself, and which generates a feeling hard to describe. The best way to understand it is to try it—and I hope you do.

Other than environmental pressures, the primary threat to the existence of the trout and salmon within the next decade will be man and his attitudes towards the implementation of stricter regulations. It has been proven time and time again that longer length limits protect a given fishery by keeping smaller fish from the creel. But the ecosystem of the habitat is protected as well by regulations prohibiting the use of live bait, which lessen the chances of introduction of harmful diseases, or of warm water species and any parasites they may carry.

It is imperative, therefore, that we exclude the smaller examples of trout and salmon from our creels, allowing them to prosper and replace any larger counterparts we happen to take. And it is equally important to protect their easily altered environment if Maine fishermen and visiting anglers are to enjoy acceptable angling in the years ahead, as we have in the past.

Today, there are more anglers looking for trout and salmon than ever before. A Memorial Day boat ride on Sebago, Moosehead, or Rangeley lake, or a visit to any one of the more popular streams or rivers, will clearly support this fact. Artificial implantation of hatchery-reared fish can only maintain a fishery at a specific level. Natural reproduction of wild fish, and the assurance that a certain percentage of the wild strain will reach the mature stage, are vital if a given water is to maintain respectable populations. The killing of smaller trout and salmon, which are easier to catch, is one of the fastest and surest ways to "kill" an individual lake or river, and ultimately the resource as well.

Professional fishery biologists who know this, and who realize that appreciable resources cannot be maintained under present size and bag quotas, are asking for longer length limits and smaller bag limits. These are being widely accepted by fishermen and fishing organizations who realize their importance to the future of the trout and salmon species. These fishermen are concerned primarily with the quality of our fisheries, not the quantity in the creel. And this should be the concern of all who partake and truly enjoy the art of angling.

The understanding of reasons for, and subsequent acceptance of, such regulations is quite apparent. Fishery personnel, like those of us who cast a fly, are only human, and can manage a certain water for a specific species and make biological assessments. But the true future and well-being of the cold water species clearly lies in our hands as well, as concerned fishermen and sportsmen.

Our trout and salmon resources will survive and prosper for the enjoyment of future anglers only if we allow it—and work to assure their prosperity.

Photo by Dave O'Connor

Chapter 2
KNOW YOUR FISH

BROOK TROUT
Salvelinus fontinalis

I have chosen to begin this chapter with the brook trout for several reasons. Primarily, selfish as it may seem, because the brookie was the first fish I ever enticed to a fly and because he remains my most cherished adversary with a fly rod.

Also, I think it is only fitting to put the brook trout in his rightful place. As king of Maine sportfish, and as the demon who baptizes most of us into this world called "fly fishing", he deserves to be in the forefront.

Still another factor makes it seem proper to start with the brookie—perhaps the most important factor of all. It is my firm conviction that no other Maine fishery has been so harshly treated—no other habitat so needlessly exploited—as that of *Salvelinus fontinalis*.

The encroachment of man upon the environment has taken its toll on the brook trout. Once the most widely distributed of any cold water sportfish in America, the brookie now has withdrawn to a last sanctuary in northern

21

Maine. I am pleased and grateful to reside in a state which can provide such a refuge and still offer the best native brook trout angling remaining in the United States.

The brook trout inhabits clean, cold lakes and ponds, which offer good supplies of oxygen and feed. Rivers and streams with rapids, agitated currents, and deep pools are also preferred.

The squaretail, as the brook trout is commonly calle.¹ in Maine, is a solitary individual, thriving in waters where no other fishery exists. Brookies are known to be the least tolerant of all sportfish within our waters. And in northern Maine, true native populations are rarely found in the same lake or pond as brown trout or landlocked salmon, two highly competitive species known for their dominant characteristics.

A member of the char family, the brookie is a heavy feeder, consuming almost anything from small trout of its own kind to chubs, small minnows, nymphs, flies, and terrestrial insects. This is a prime reason why they are such an advantageous attraction to even the most inexperienced of fly fishermen; compared to other cold water fish, the omnivorous brook trout is relatively easy to catch.

Prior to the turn of the century, native brook trout were found in many Maine waters. But man's cutting and polluting of the environment caused whole populations to disappear from southern waters with alarming speed. By the mid-1930s, true native populations were rare in the once-prime habitat south of Augusta. And heavy stocking programs were needed to keep the brookie population at fishable levels.

Today, native populations are found in scattered, hard-to-reach beaver bogs and little-known ponds in southern Maine. But such places are indeed hard to find, and are usually kept secret by knowing anglers. For all practical circumstances, the native brook trout is gone from southern Maine.

The northern waters, therefore, remain the last sanctuary of Maine's native brook trout fishery. Fortunately for the species, and for fly fishermen, this vast region is largely under private ownership. Were it not, the brook trout fishery as a whole might have been exhausted long ago—although many biological minds state otherwise.

For the most part, angling for the brook trout is still good in most areas of northern and western Maine. In many places, it could actually be called excellent. Productivity in the creel depends a great deal upon fishing pressure, the angler's skill and knowledge of the species, and certain natural circumstances affecting behavior of the trout themselves. (Success to some degree is usually available in most places throughout the open season for fly fishermen of all calibers, however.)

Photo by Maine Fish and Wildlife Dept.

Brook Trout *Salvelinus fontinalis*

A list of famed and popular brook trout waters can be found in Chapter 6. But the angler should not hesitate to wet his line in waters less famous, for such habitats often prove highly cooperative.

As stated earlier, the brookie forages for feed constantly. Flies tied to resemble his desired edibles often produce the best results. Except during times of sporadic or regular emergences of natural insects (only about 25 percent of the angling season), the brookie feeds beneath the surface. Because of this, wet patterns will take more, and larger, fish. Dry flies also take their share, however, and the use of dry patterns is more popular with the average fly fisherman. We will discuss some of the best patterns, wet and dry, a little later on.

Compared with other trout and salmon, the brook trout is a short-lived species. Mortality among the young fry is extremely high, and heavy fishing pressure takes a majority of the adult fish. These two factors could very well be the prime challenges to the survival of native populations in the years ahead.

A century ago, when our fly fishing forefathers were creeling native brook trout in the five- and six-pound class with regularity from the famed Rangeley Lake area, little thought was given to the age of such fish or their importance to a certain water. Without a doubt, however, these lunkers were the result of a decade's growth, and the taking of such specimens was a severe blow to the lake's reproductive capabilities. The proof is evident in the way Rangeley's brook trout population declined betwen 1870 and 1900, when the landlocked salmon emerged as the principal fishery there.

In most Maine waters today, a six-year-old brook trout is considered old and, in the majority of our lakes and ponds, extremely rare. Trout two and three years of age make up the bulk of the catches, with individuals varying between 10 and 14 inches long, depending upon the habitat.

Another interesting, and alarming, fact is the mortality of young trout fry. The brookie spawns in the fall, usually from mid-September into December, in Maine. Populations normally inhabiting lakes and ponds seek cold tributaries, but if none are available, they will nest on gravel bars and reefs where cold, clean water can cleanse the eggs. Trout already inhabiting brooks, streams, and rivers usually move into smaller feeder brooks, but nesting in year-round pools or riffle areas is also common.

It is the female who constructs the 4- to 12-inch-deep pit, or *redd*, while the males fight vigorously for the privilege of courting her. One biological reference was witness to a battle during which two males actually locked jaws and rolled away down a riffle area.

Unlike most other fish, the female brook trout does not lay a great number of eggs—and this is the alarming factor. A two-pound adult female may produce as few as 1,000 eggs; a two-pound white perch, by comparison, may drop as many as 250,000.

Complicating this infant mortality are the heavy losses which occur during the first year of life. Of 10,000 fry born in a given spring, no more than 500 are expected to live to the end of their first year. Of this original 10,000, only one or two will live to be six years of age.

Perhaps we should remember this the next time we creel an impresive squaretail. Hopefully, more of us will take to the catch-and-release, or fishing-for-sport, concept of angling in the years ahead to help preserve this noble species.

At the present time, the native brook trout is holding its own in northern Maine. And heavy stocking efforts are making hatchery-reared specimens available in southern areas. In 1977, 750 lakes and ponds listing the brook trout as their principal fishery were included in a census by the Maine Department of Inland Fisheries and Wildlife. Hopefully, careful management and consideration from landowners and fishermen can ensure that this number will not deteriorate in the years ahead.

The true native brook trout is an impressive example of Mother Nature's creative skill. Because of my fondness for them, I would personally call them the most "pleasing-to-the-eye" of all Maine game fish. The brookie is truly a beauty in the opinion of most fly fishermen—and for good reason!

The sides of these beauties are dotted with bright red spots, surrounded by blue aureoles. The dorsal fin has 10 or 11 distinguishable soft rays. The anal fin usually has nine rays.

The pectoral, ventral, and anal fins are reddish, trimmed with a fairly prominent white edge. The overall body, especially the back and the upper sides, is covered with wavy designs called *vermiculations*. The belly is creamy white on most females, while the males often display a bright orange, especially during spawning. I have taken brookies in late September on Northern ponds, and they are truly pleasing to the eye.

Overall, the brook trout has more coloration than any other native Maine trout or salmon. Only the rainbow trout surpasses it for aesthetic value—although some landlocked salmon purists may argue otherwise.

The flesh of the brook trout is normally rich orange or pink, characteristic of the char family. This trait can vary due to habitat, however, and whitish flesh is common with hatchery-reared trout.

As for the taste? Henry Hill Collins, in his book, *The Complete Field Guide to American Wildlife*, describes the "best breakfast of all" as being a "panful of fresh Brook Trout by a streamside fire."

Not much more need be said about the native brook trout.

LANDLOCKED SALMON
Salmo salar

Few fresh water fish can rival the fighting magnificence of the landlocked salmon. Without a doubt they are the most aerobatic and aggressive battlers on a fly rod. And, because of this fact, they have for decades been a popular attraction of Maine fly fishermen.

Other than the brook trout, the landlocked salmon has the closest kinship with the Maine fly fishing fraternity. More flies have been conceived and tied to entice this fighter to the hook than any other salmonid. Our forefathers thought them to be a mystical fish—eventually they replaced the squaretail as King of Maine sportfish in the minds of many anglers.

The landlocked salmon remains a mystical individual, as he was 100 years ago, drawing millions of anglers to Down East lakes and rivers annually. In many places, he is the most sought-after species, and I feel he will eventually overtake the brook trout as the most popular fishery throughout Maine.

The landlocked is a native of Maine. Originally, they were found in only four lakes: West Grand Lake in Washington County, Green Lake in Hancock County, Sebec Lake in Penobscot County, and Sebago Lake in Cumberland County (the most famous of them all).

Since 1875, however, the landlocked has been widely introduced and stocked throughout the state. They are now found in more than 250 lakes and ponds, although this number does not include rivers and streams where the landlocked is known to exist. The actual number of waters now housing landlocked salmon is impressive indeed. There is no question that Maine

Landlocked Salmon *Salmo salar*

maintains and manages the largest sport fishery of landlocked salmon in the world.

Putting their fighting abilities aside, the landlocked is a beautiful fish, although quite unlike any other Maine species. The back is a dark blue-green on most specimens, although many appear black. The sides are spotted with distinquishable "X" markings which lead down and fade against the small cycloid scaled sides, characteristically silver color. The belly is creamy white, the fins dark and soft-rayed, the adipose fin usually small.

Salmon accept all flies readily, but streamers, bucktails, and dry flies (in that order) are most commonly used by Maine fly fishermen. Streamers and small bucktails are more popular in lakes and ponds, and on rivers early in the season, while dry flies are almost always used in those rivers housing salmon during the emergence of important insects. As a rule, the average fisherman associates the landlocked with the sinking fly, but the floating imitation is a valuable weapon during May and June when May flies, caddis flies, and stone flies are emerging on Maine rivers and streams.

Most famed and renowned fly patterns designed especially for landlocked salmon were indeed streamers, bucktails, and wet flies. Few dry patterns were designed specifically with this salmonid in mind—but Maine salmon follow the brook trout's feeding characteristics, accepting feed when and where it is most plentiful. So, once predominent hatches start to show over the water, landlocked salmon, like the brookie, will readily rise to the surface to feed.

Salmon have a history of growing to impressive sizes in Maine. The largest landlocked ever taken on a rod and reel came from Sebago Lake in 1907 and weighed 22½ pounds; it has yet to be topped.

It is rumored that an example weighing 36 pounds was taken the same year from Sebago by fishery personnel while seining salmon for stripping. This is unofficial, although highly possible for that time.

According to Maine Department of Inland Fisheries and Wildlife data, the majority of salmon taken by fishermen today average between three and six years of age. The following table is an average length graph of salmon found in Maine waters under normal habitat conditions. It will not apply to every water in the state, although it is not far out of line.

AGE		AVERAGE LENGTH
1		5.9
2	(illegal)	11.6
. . . .		
3		15.2
4	(commonly taken)	18.1
5		20.3
6		22.2
. . . .		
7		23.5
8	(rarely taken over age 7	25.2
9		27.9

Spawning of Maine salmon takes place usually between mid-October and late November. Adult fish may move into tributary waters by the first week of September if a good flow of water is available. The run can be postponed several weeks, however, if water is unusually low.

Females construct several egg pits by turning on their sides and flapping vigorously with their caudal penduncle and caudal fin. Eggs from the female and milt from the male are deposited simultaneously, after which the pit is gently covered with gravel by the female.

Unlike Atlantic salmon, who often remain in spawning rivers after this ritual is completed, the landlocked usually returns to his year-round home, whether lake or pond. If large tributary rivers or streams are not available, the landlocked will spawn on lake shoals at the mouths of outlets and small tributary brooks. But ideal locations offer swift riffle areas with gravel bottoms to supply the eggs with oxgyen and a clean environment.

It should be mentioned that the fall-run landlocked salmon is an extremely uncooperative angling partner. He eats little or nothing at all during the move upstream and during the spawning proceedings. Making him accept a fly can be a frustrating task. It can sometimes take nearly 200 casts into a pool or riffle area before a salmon accepts a fly during this fall-run period. This fact, however, should not deter the fly fisherman, even the novice, from fall salmon fishing. Quite the contrary. Fishing in September is one of the most enjoyable and challenging of angling experiences. And it can he highly rewarding, even given the reluctance of our adversary.

According to data from the Maine Department of Inland Fisheries and Wildlife, female salmon usually spawn for the first time at age four or five. Males, on the other hand, mature and participate at age three or four. As much as 70% of each run is composed of salmon spawning for the first time.

If we look again at the table on page   , we see that the majority of fish available to fall fishermen measure between 15.2 and 22.2 inches. An impressive reward in any fisherman's book!

Salmon fry emerge from their gravel nest between the last week of May and mid-June. These young, called *parr*, will remain in the river or stream of their birth for one or two years before moving downstream to a lake or pond. During this time, small insects and aquatic organisms serve as their main food supply. But after the move into open water, forage fish, particularly the smelt, becomes their staple diet. When the smelt is not readily available, the salmon will forage on aquatic insects, other small fish, and terrestrial insects. This tells us that the landlocked is susceptible to a variety of fly patterns.

Spring fishing for landlocked salmon can be a rewarding venture. On many Maine lakes, smelts start to move into tributary waters to spawn just before, during, or immediately after ice-out. Salmon follow them to the mouths of rivers, streams and brooks with the intention of filling their empty bellies after a long hard winter. Casting some of the popular smelt imitation flies into deep pools or riffle areas at this time can be extremely productive. Trolling large tandem-hooked streamer flies where these tributaries enter a lake or pond is often successful as well. Such tactics will be discussed more closely later on.

The landlocked is not characteristically a deep-dwelling fish. In lakes and ponds, they normally are found from 10-35 feet below the surface. But if feed is difficult to find, they will go much deeper—sometimes as deep as 100 feet.

In rivers and large streams, salmon hang to the deep pools where water is turbulent, oxygen supply is good, and feed is constantly flowing downstream. In the warmer months, the riffle areas are popular for the same reasons.

Often, salmon will be found lying on the downstream side of a large rock or boulder, or waiting at the head of a pool where the current consistently supplies their needs.

Success in such places depends on a great deal upon how and where an angler presents his offering and how he works the pattern in the water. We will discuss some of the favorite Maine salmon fishing techniques in Chapter 3.

BROWN TROUT
Salmo trutta

The brown trout, not a native of Maine, was introduced here for the first time at Branch Lake in Ellsworth in 1885. Maine holds the distinction of being the third state in America to introduce the brown trout to its waters; New York and Michigan were first (in 1883).

Since the turn of the century *Salmo trutta* has been introduced in 42 of the United States—all but three introductions were highly successful. In Canada, he is now found in nine of the twelve provinces—and this hardy fish has been planted also in South America, Africa, India, Australia, and New Zealand. Not bad for a fish which had a native range restricted to Europe and Western Asia a little more than one hundred years ago! Through transplant by man, the brown trout now is one of the most available freshwater sportfish in the world. And one of the most popular!

In Maine, heavy stocking efforts prior to 1930 saw the brown trout rapidly introduced to an impressive number of southern and central lakes and ponds. The move was a highly controversial one at the time, for reasons we will discover later. But today, nearly 180 Maine lakes, ponds, rivers, and streams either hold or are stocked annually with brown trout. And there is every indication that this number will increase in the years ahead as the brown becomes more popular.

The brown is a member of the salmonid family. Unlike the salmon, however, he can withstand higher water temperatures, will accept a wider range of feed, and is a more competitive fighter for spawning territory. He is far more adaptable to a broader variety of living conditions than the brook trout or landlocked salmon. And because of this pliability, he is often a threat to existing populations of native trout and salmon.

At the turn of the century, however, little was known of the brown's competitive and domineering spirit. Fishery biologists believed the brown to be a great asset to the Maine sportfish family. Stocking efforts continued with zest from 1885 to 1930, when the outcry from sportsmen demanded more research concerning these fish and their possible threats to native populations.

By the early 1930s, Maine fishery personnel had done their job—and done it well. It was discovered that the brown's versatile characteristics and strong will for survival could allow him, in time, to dominate a lake completely, even though landlocked salmon or brook trout had been the principal fishery at the time of introduction.

Since that discovery, it has been department policy to stock brown trout only in waters where they pose no threat to brook trout or landlocked salmon

Photo by Maine Fish and Wildlife Dept.

Brown Trout *Salmo trutta*

populations. Or in waters where stocking is required to *maintain* the fishery.

Although not quite as aesthetic as the brookie, the brown is an impressive looking salmonid, very pleasing to the eye. The body is covered with small cycloid scales, like the landlocked, except for the head, which is smooth to the touch.

As fry, the body is marked by nine or ten dark "parr" marks which fade as the fish matures into a fingerling. Occasionally, though not often in Maine, these parr marks will remain with the fish throughout its life.

Along the brown's body are eight fins; dorsal, adipose, caudal, anal, a pair of ventral fins attached to the lower belly, and a pair of pectoral fins located behind the gills. The anal fin is trimmed with a thin edge of black and a broader line of white. As fingerlings, the dorsal fin is forked, becoming square or slightly concave in shape as the fish matures.

The mature brown is characteristically dark brown along the back, mixed with shades of olive green, gold and yellow down the sides, particularly below the lateral line. Superimposed on these colors is a mixture of black and sometimes red spots edged with haloes of light blue; the red spots are absent on many immature fish or small adults. The dorsal and adipose fins are also spotted, as are the gill covers. The reamining fins are typically yellow, and unmarked.

Coloration of the brown varies a great deal depending upon habitat. I have taken, from southern Maine lakes, browns resembling landlocked salmon to such a degree that the difference in vomerine teeth and spotted adipose fins were the only clues to their true identity. The majority of browns taken from rivers and streams seem to hold to the characteristic coloration and their identity is not difficult to distinguish.

The brown is a fighting individual with an unrelenting reluctance to be creeled. He is a strong fighter who alternately breaks water and makes long underwater runs once hooked. He is not as aerobatic on the line as the landlocked, but what he lacks in finesse, he makes up for in power and spirit.

Anglers seeking to challenge the brown in rivers and streams with riffle areas and deep pools should be equipped with a rod possessing some backbone—a rod with a "stiff action." An eight-foot rod is good, but an 8½-footer will enable the angler to get his fly to those "untouchable" lies just out of reach of smaller rods.

Tapered leaders are a must for successful *Salmo trutta* anglers. A fair rule to remember is: the leader should be as long as the rod. If you use an eight-foot rod, use at least an eight-foot leader, and so on. Experimenting with different lengths will soon indicate which is best for you, however. For my personal use, the longer the leader, the better, but rarely do fly leaders exceed ten feet.

When fishing for the brown, I normally use an 8½-foot graphite rod with a nine-foot leader tied to a number six line—the combination works well for me. However, I believe that the length of the leader should not vary more than twelve inches from the rod length. Lengthy leaders can, unless in experienced hands, hamper a proper presentation, essential when challenging this finicky individual. This leader rule is good to remember when in search of any sportfish.

High quality leaders with 1½- to 2-pound tippets are recommended for browns in streams and small rivers. If strong current is to be fought, switch to 2½-pound tippets.

When conditions permit, the brown prefers to gorge himself on floating matter rather than edibles beneath the surface. Because of this fact, *Salmon trutta* is a favorite among dry fly purists. I think it is safe to say that the majority of brown trout taken on Maine rivers and streams each year are taken on floating flies. Proper presentation and placement of the artificial, as well as a natural drift, are necessary requirements. And it is often required to match the emerging natural for success. The brown is extremely cautious when accepting surface forage, and productivity demands that all factors be precise.

Being the carnivorous creatures they are, brown trout can be enticed to a number of artificial patterns other than those which float. Some of the best ones imitate grasshoppers, ants, flies, small fish, crayfish, and various other bugs. Entomologists believe, however, that such aquatic and terrestrial creatures supply only about ten percent of the brown's needs.

The caddis fly supplies this much alone. Over much of Maine, the May fly, and various family offshoots, are the favorite food of the brown, supplying up to 80 percent of their feed during the open water months. Noted 19th century fishing writer, fly tier, and angler Fredric Halford put it this way: "Floating food is caviar; but underwater food is beef to the brown trout."

Knowing this, the brown trout fisherman should arm himself with a variety of fly patterns, both nympth and dry fashion, to resemble these families in all stages. If this is done, streamers and bucktails are unnecessary box filler. Although 510 different kinds of May flies are known to exist in North America, a well-selected assortment of artificials works best on brown trout in Maine. We will discuss those flies and make our selection in Chapter Five.

Brown trout mature at a slightly younger age than landlocked salmon; it is common for both sexes to become sexually mature in their second year, although females may wait until their third year.

Some time in late October, the female moves into tributary rivers or streams, selecting a spawning site with a gravel bottom near a riffle area, or at the lower end of a pool where circulation and aeration from the water is constantly available.

While she prepares the egg pit(s), usually measuring six inches deep by one foot long, the male stays close by—one biological reference states: "about a foot to the rear." But the male is often kept busy protecting his mate, and the spawning territory, from small yearlings who often become stimulated by uncontrollable desire.

Eggs and milt are deposited simultaneously, as with all salmonids. Once the female is "spent"—after filling perhaps two or three pits and dropping several thousand eggs, the male often goes off the court another mate while the female covers the hummock, her spawning finished for the season.

The young hatch in late winter or early spring (from late March to mid-April), depending upon habitat. As with the brook trout, the mortality rate among the young is extremely high. From fry to yearling, as much as 90 percent may be lost. Two-year olds may suffer a 50 percent loss, and out of 1,000 eggs in a complete redd, only three or perhaps four fish will reach four years of age.

Compared to other salmonids, the brown is a short-lived species. Average life expectancy in Maine is about three years; four- and five-year olds are rare. The oldest brown ever examined in Maine was ten years old. This fact, along with the mortality among the young, is a clear indication of the brown trout's will for survival. His domineering spirit and love for a floating fly makes him one of fly fishing's most cherished quarries.

Browns grow to impressive sizes in Maine. This, along with their fighting spirit and aesthetic value, makes them highly attractive to most anglers. The largest brown ever recorded in Maine weighed 19 pounds, 7 ounces, and was taken from Sebago Lake in 1958. Although such specimens are rare today, examples in the 9-, 10- and 11-pound range are taken from several large lakes on occasion. But the average lake brown is probably closer to three or four pounds, with five and six pound examples being considered trophy size.

Those specimens confined to rivers and streams are relatively smaller. But two-pound examples are taken on several Maine watersheds; one- to one-and-one-half-pound browns measuring between 14 and 18 inches would be considered average.

Salmon trutta are intelligent fish. They have the keenest sense of smell and the sharpest eyesight of any sportfish inhabiting Maine waters, and their strategic traits make them somewhat difficult for the average angler to hook with a fly rod. The creeling of a mature adult is a good sign of a caster's skill, indeed. For it is these two- and three-year-olds which have acquired the traits that have made the brown trout the most respected sportfish available to the fly fisherman.

It has long been the belief of Maine fishery biologists that the brown is a poor investment for any water in terms of returns to the fisherman's hourly angling effort, especially if that water is capable of supporting native trout or salmon instead. Although there are no records available comparing the hourly angling ratios on these fish, I feel that, considering the brown's delicate disposition and reluctance to accept any other than the best delivered and matching imitation, and considering also the popularity of the brook trout and landlocked salmon, the brown is low on the ladder in terms of returns to the fisherman. It is doubtful, therefore, that this fighting individual will be introduced to many waters, or become the predominant Maine game fish, as long as landlocked salmon and brook trout maintain their present status.

It is personally felt, however, that southern Maine will see more and more brown trout introduced to certain waters in the years ahead, as the less tolerant trout and salmon come face to face with increased fishing pressure and environmental challenges. It will be many years before western and northern Maine waters require that their brown trout fishery offer appreciable angling resources. Eventual introduction of the fish in selected waters, however, I believe to be inevitable.

RAINBOW TROUT
Salmo gairdneri

Of all the fish inhabiting Maine's cold water lakes, ponds, and rivers, the rainbow trout is unquestionably the most colorful. They are noted as being jumpers and headstrong fighters once hooked and they readily accept flies, particularly those that float. Although limited in abundance in Maine, the

Photo by Maine Fish and Wildlife Dept.

Rainbow Trout *Salmo gairdneri*

"bow" is truly one of the most prized and challenging fish a fly fisherman can ever hope to meet.

The first rainbow trout introduced in Maine waters were from the McCloud River area in California. A total of 50,000 fingerlings (Maine received them as eggs) were stocked in a number of unspecified waters throughout the state in 1880. By 1896, Maine was producing her own rainbow stock at the then-active Caribou Fish Hatchery. Fish from that rearing station were released in the Aroostook and Meduxnekeag Rivers, both in Aroostook County, in that year. Records of other stockings in that period are virtually nonexistent.

Records do show, however, that rainbow trout were stocked in Auburn Lake and Taylor Pond, both in Auburn, and in Wilson Pond in Monmouth, as early as 1902. By the 1930s, the rainbow had been introduced to more than 20 Maine lakes and ponds. Such familiar ponds as Little Sebago, Kezar Lake, and Wilson's Pond in Acton had received them prior to this date. But they were also stocked in the Saco River near Hiram, the Little Ossipee River near Newfield, and the Ossipee River at Kezar Falls. They were released in upper stretches of the Androscoggin River in Oxford County in 1927, and in the Royal River in Cumberland County a year later. The rainbow was unable to sustain itself in those waters, however, and is gone today.

The original concept of rainbow introduction was to supply a sport fishery in waters where landlocked salmon and brook trout would not be feasible, or in waters where these two species had disappeared. By the 1940s, however, it was noted that the rainbow's characteristics were making it difficult to establish self-sustaining populations in many Maine lakes and rivers. If a rainbow fishery was to be maintained, therefore, a heavy stocking program was needed to supply our own fingerlings.

In addition, raising rainbows was proving hazardous to other fish populations at the hatchery. Unless another rearing site could be built exclusively for the rainbow, at a great cost to Maine sportsmen, the project would have to cease—and it did, in the middle of the 1940s.

In the early 1970s, it was again decided to try establishing the rainbow in a number of Maine waters. Some 43,000 eggs were obtained from the Fish Genetics Laboratory in Wyoming and deposited in seventeen lakes and rivers located throughout the state. Only one, the Kennebec River in Somerset County can boast of a self-sustaining rainbow trout fishery today.

The failure to establish the rainbow after such an extensive trial period, coupled with rising costs at the hatchery, forced a decision that 1979 would be the last year of rainbow stocking throughout the state. Experiments have indicated that existing populations except in the Kennebec, have not yet reproduced or firmly established themselves within their habitat. Within a decade, Maine will be barren of any rainbow trout fishery, unless the Kennebec continues to maintain its self-sustaining population. And Maine will truly be losing an impressive fighting sportfish.

The rainbow is a member of the trout family and is the only cold water sportfish in Maine which spawns in the spring—from mid-April to late May, depending upon habitat. Due to the warming of the water at this time, incubation time is relatively short, the fry emerging from their gravel beds within 30 to 35 days (as early as the first of June). Mortality rate among the young is high, only one or two individuals out of each 2,000 fry reaching the age of two years.

As fly fishing attractions, rainbow are among the best. They possess a high-strung, fighting spirit, and are known for their leaping antics once hooked by the fisherman. Compared with the landlocked salmon, I would say they jump as much as, if not more than, our native salmonid.

The rainbow is traditionally known for its love of floating flies. But in the Kennebec, for example, bucktails and streamers take their share as well. In the spring, when river waters are high and strong, a sinking fly line, preferably with weight forward taper, is recommended. With streamers or bucktails, it is necessary to cast sharply up and across the river with a rapid retrieve to prevent slack in the line.

Once the river has subsided, floating flies, used with a floating line and sturdy leader, produce the majority of fish. Some popular and productive rainbow patterns and their use techniques will be discussed later on.

THE SMALLMOUTH BASS
Micropterus dolomieui
and
THE LARGEMOUTH BASS
Micropterus salmoides

Many fishermen are unaware that the smallmouth and largemouth bass are not native inhabitants of Maine. The smallmouth arrived first, some time just after the Civil War era, while the largemouth has been here only since the early 1900s. Two of the earliest stockings of largemouths took place in Long Pond and Messalonskee Lake, both in the Belgrade Lakes region of Kennebec County, in 1940.

Once scorned by the fly fishing fraternity and feared as a threat to native salmon and trout populations, these members of the sunfish family are now highly respected for their fighting spirit and impressive power on the line. This is particularly true of the smallmouth, who is often credited with being the better fighter of the two species.

Unlike the largemouth, who prefers a warm habitat, the smallmouth is better suited to lakes, ponds, and rivers with relatively cold, clean water and gravelly or rocky bottoms and shorelines. A good example would be Sebago Lake, a famed cold water salmon lake which also has a healthy population of smallmouth bass.

Both species are carnivores, feeding on just about anything that moves in or on top of the water. Due to this fact, bass have been attractive to an increasing number of flycasters since the early 1960s. The harsh attitudes towards them,

Photo by Maine Fish and Wildlife Dept.

Largemouth Bass *Micropterus salmoides*

which had swollen out of proportion primarily due to concern for native fish populations, have now subsided to a great degree, and the bass is now an accepted member of the gamefish fraternity.

Although the majority of fly fishermen believe that the bass family should be controlled and managed so as not to endanger Maine's trout or salmon fishery, most anglers feel that he *does* have a place in Maine's sportfishing future.

One reason these two species have gained in popularity is that they offer challenge and sport during the warmer months of summer, when trout and salmon activity is apt to be slow. This is particularly true on many southern and central Maine trout and salmon ponds, which become over-crowded with other water recreationalists once the summer weather has arrived. On lakes and ponds where water-skiing and high-speed motorboats are heavily utilized, trout and salmon often seek deeper waters to avoid the commotion. Bass, on the other hand, especially largemouth, hold to the shallow weed-covered coves and shorelines and offer spectacular sport and action.

Both species will accept flies with zest. Dry flies are best during the early morning or late afternoon hours when the water is calm. They must be worked hard to create a disturbance on the placid surface to draw the fish's attention if action is to be expected. Small plastic or wooden "poppers" attached to a bass tapered line often produces better results.

Both largemouth and smallmouth attack bucktails and streamer flies with relish and, without a doubt, more fish are taken with these two designs than with any others. Like the dry fly or "popper", however, the bucktail or streamer must be worked hard, with good solid jerks, to work properly.

Photo by Maine Fish and Wildlife Dept.

Chapter 3
TECHNIQUE—A KEY TO SUCCESS

There is an ongoing debate among fly fishermen: which is more important, the *selection* of our artificials or the *presentation* of them? It is a lively debate, for it cannot be answered easily or simply. In many areas of the country, particularly where the brown trout is considered king, anglers argue that both are important for action; this is basicaly true, even here in Maine.

In many areas of the East, especially in Vermont, New York and Pennsylvania where trout have a tendency to be overly selective due to rich insect life and large hatches, many fly fishermen consider *selection* of artificials—their size, coloration, and resemblance to the specific natural—more important than presentation. The technique with which these flies are used is basic, with much of the success coming from matching the natural with an artificial twin.

As many resident and frequent visiting fly fishermen know, however, fishing in Maine is often unorthodox when compared to other areas of the country. As you will discover in Chapter 5, while the choice of artificials *is* important on Maine waters, the technique with which we deliver them is significant for success—in many cases, more so than the actual resemblance of the fly to the natural model.

Several factors substantiate this statement. Consider that Maine rivers, streams, and ponds do not contain as rich an insect ecosystem as other parts of the country. Our May fly, caddis fly, and stone fly hatches are much smaller and last for a shorter period of time than those in Vermont, New York, and waters of the West. For this reason, Maine trout and landlocked salmon are characteristically less selective. Other factors, such as water conditions and temperatures, water clarity, and other available insect and terrestrial life, however, make our technique and delivery of artificials highly important and challenging.

I have always said that, before he can expect to catch fish consistently, a fly fisherman must know how to cast properly. All the artificials known to the fishing fraternity will not produce the desired results unless delivered in such a manner so as not to disturb the prey, and so that they float and drift naturally and as freely as possible on the water surface. The angler can worry later about "matching the hatch" and catching the trophies. For without proper presentation, drift, and retrieve, his chances of a worthy battle are small.

DRY FLIES

The Dry Fly Upstream

The most popular method of utilizing the dry fly in streams and rivers is an upstream, or an up-and-slightly-across-stream, fashion. This tactic is universally accepted as the most feasible casting approach in such habitat for a number of reasons.

Trout and salmon nearly always position themselves facing the current. This allows them greater mobility, and keeps them looking in the direction from which the majority of their food comes. I have personally observed specimens lying horizontally behind boulders and submerged logs, but they usually face the flow.

This gives a great advantage to stream fishermen. Not only does this trait restrict the fish's peripheral vision, but it allows the angler opportunities to get closer to obvious lies, thus allowing him to present his offering with less chance of disturbing the water surface.

Another asset with upstream casting is that when the offering is taken, the hook is pulled into the mouth of a rising trout or salmon rather than away from the fish, as is commonly experienced when casting downstream.

When a fly caster is working a Maine stream, he should remember these basics: work slowly, carefully, and diligently, and be as accurate and natural with the imitation as possible. Keep in mind the sensitivity of the habitat. It takes very little motion on the water's surface, and even less below the surface, to disturb a trout or salmon.

Long casts, for example, are impressive but are usually our downfall. Nearly always, fish can be caught within thirty feet of your position—in most cases, closer than twenty feet. Shorter casts are not only easier to deliver, but reduce the amount of drag; this is a great help when working powerful current areas. If you receive no action within these distances, there is a good chance that you're working too fast and have already spooked the fish in that area.

Along with delivering short, delicate casts, you must wade a stream slowly, almost at a snail's pace. Enter the stream at a location far below the pool or stretch you intend to fish. Keep low to the water's surface to restrict your silhouette and avoid casting a shadow over the fish.

From your first casting position, carefully scan the pool before going to work. Locate the best lies and holding areas, and decide in your mind the best way to present your offering with the least amount of disturbance. Make a series of casts into the general vicinity, always bringing the fly to rest four or five feet above the actual holding area. Immediately retrieve as much line as you can without maneuvering the artificial; allow it to drift as long as possible downstream. Some of the best fish are taken as the pattern finishes its drift and is ready to be retrieved and recast.

The ideal cast upstream is on an angle—upstream and to the right or upstream and to the left. Presentations quartered in this manner reveal only a small section of the leader, none of the line, and allow the fly to drift over the fish with little drag and in the most natural fashion, which is what we're after. This technique is particularly deadly when trout or salmon are rising in a specific area, especially if we are quick and accurate enough to get our fly into a rise with little disturbance.

Casting directly upstream is a good tactic to master, but is most difficult to conduct perfectly with each presentation, particularly in extremely fast or powerful water. It is not quite as difficult in slower eddy and riffle areas, but excess drag on the line, causing the fly to drift too rapidly and erratically downstream, is the main problem. Also, fishermen working directly against the current have a tendency to misjudge distance; leaders and line often land over the fish. By the time the fly is in the proper position, the trout or salmon is gone and it will be several minutes before he will have settled down and become willing to feed again.

In extremely turbulent water, this really doesn't matter much, since the vision of fish inhabiting such areas is greatly distorted by the broken surface. The direct upstream cast is best used in such areas rather than in placid pools, since distrubances of the surface by line and fly are "lost in the shuffle." Experience shows the up-and-quartering-across-stream tactic to be more important for the majority of Maine conditions. Some of the larger rivers, however, require a direct upstream presentation to entice fish away from a mid-stream lie.

When working dry flies in rough water, whether casting upstream or down, I prefer patterns that float high. And, because I know my quarry's vision is not up to par in such waters, I don't hesitate to utilize a fly one size bigger than the natural. I often start with a 10 Wulff or Irresistible pattern unless a specific natural is emerging. In those cases, I match coloration and size, then go to larger sizes in the same shade if action is not received.

In calmer stretches and particularly deep, clear pools, size consideration is reversed. I match the natural if possible, but if the offering is being hit but not accepted, a smaller fly is offered on a smaller tippet. Some excellent calm water flies for Maine rivers and streams include the Cahills and Hendricksons (both Light and Dark), the March Brown, the Quill Gordon, the Mosquito, and the Red Quill. Usually, sizes between 12 and 16 will do the job.

The Dry Fly Downstream

At Upper Dam on the Rapid River, one of my favorite tactics is to stand on the dam and cast a high-floating dry fly directly downstream. The water is fast and powerful in that area, and working a floating imitation upstream can be a dilemma due to the movement of the water.

This is a productive tactic on many fast stretches, particularly where riffles and rapids empty into small pools where casting a fly is not possible. Not only is wading with the current easier than wading against it, but casting directly downstream puts your fly over the fish before the leader or line; this is the greatest asset in fishing downstream.

Several factors govern when a fly should be worked downstream. Wind and sun are two determining ingredients, but on-the-spot calculations are best. Undercut banks, water too deep to wade or out of upstream casting reach, stretches overgrown with bank growth, the upstream side of submerged logs and boulders, and bridge abutments and their edges—all are areas which hold acceptable fish, and where a downstream fly will produce results.

The best tactic is to rip off access line and make a short, forward cast, bringing your offering to rest way short of its mark. Gently release more line, letting the fly drift naturally over the fish. Long, fine-tipped leaders are best for this maneuver and, when the acceptance comes, chances are you will be setting the hook away from the fish; do not overreact!

The Dry Fly On Ponds

Most fly fishermen start their apprenticeship on trout ponds. It is one of the easiest parts of the art, and one of the most productive—and it is a good way to see what fly fishing is all about. Unfortunately, however, action on the surface in these areas is received for a short perod of time compared to action below the surface.

The bulk of productivity is seen during the early morning and late afternoon and evening hours from mid-May through late June. Certain May fly and caddis fly genuses emerge during the early afternoon hours, however, and production is good at those times. Sporadic insect hatches, and terrestrial life as well, keep trout coming to the surface throughout the season in the evening if conditions are right. But productivity is reduced considerably over much of the state once warm weather has arrived.

When a May fly or some other important insect emergence takes place on a Maine trout pond, fishing is relatively easy. Match the natural in size and coloration and you'll get results. Once your offering has come to rest on the water, give it some life, with periodic twitches of the rod, imitating an emerging dun drying its wings. No finer time can be found.

Once the predominent hatches have dispersed, however, fishing in ponds becomes a challenge. Then the angler must locate the spring holes, or work near inlets which bring cool, aerated water into the pond. Trout will seek these sanctuaries during warm weather, not only for the cooler temperatures, but for food as well.

Generally speaking, the most productive hours with dry flies during warm-weather periods are just before daybreak, before the sun hits the waters and drives the trout down, and late in the afternoon and evening, once the sun has started to set. Most of us prefer a placid surface, but a slight wind chop is often beneficial; it not only distorts the trout's vision, but fish are not as selective when the surface is broken—it offers them a sense of security as well.

The deadliest cast is to a trout's rise, when the fish is still in his feeding pattern close to the surface. A well-executed cast, with the fly placed in the rise, is, in most cases, a sure bet for action and is a tactic many warm-weather pond fishermen rely on for productivity. It is equally as productive during an insect hatch, although such accuracy and timing is often not required due to the heavy amount of surface activity.

When trout do not appear to be rising in the pond itself, the angler's best bet is to anchor about 100 feet off an inlet, cast into the riffle areas, and let his offering drift naturally into the pond. Trout often congregate in these riffle and fast-water areas, awaiting food.

During warm-weather periods, when fish are found in these locations, small midges, mosquitos, and such constitute a large percentage of forage, so utilize a similar imitation on a fine tippet. It may be difficult to keep an eye on them, but they will produce the best results.

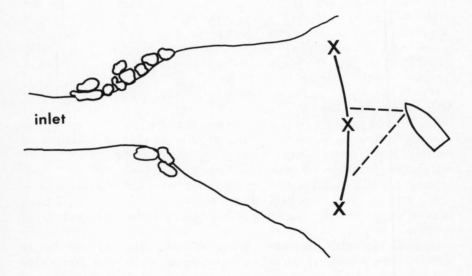

inlet

This diagram shows an inlet where cooler water will enter a warm water pond once primary hatches have ceased. Fish will lie off the mouths of these areas, waiting for the insect life to come to them. Anchor about 100 feet from the inlet, and cast inward on an upstream or quartering angle.

Spring holes in remote trout ponds, of course, are the cherished secrets of every fly fisherman. They are gold mines of activity, and will produce results even when all else fails. When the entire pond is quiet, trout, particularly small fish, will often rise to the surface for food around such areas. These small fish seem to make up the bulk of the catch once water temperatures start to rise, for larger specimens then have a tendency to stay near the bottom where larger and more filling feed is available.

It can be difficult to find spring holes. It often takes several trips to a specific pond to precisely locate them; many are in deep areas, although they can be found close to shore and in shallow water in the smaller bodies of water. A depth thermometer offers considerable aid, but close observation and the noting of continued productive areas during warm weather will give their locations away as well. Once a spring hole has been discovered, landmarks should be noted—these areas will continue to be productive summer after summer.

There are many artificial patterns which are productive during non-emergence periods. The Black Gnat is one of the best; the Mosquito is another. The midge is popular, but I have found that nearly any floating pattern resembling a specific natural or terrestrial insect is apt to produce results. Small grasshopper flies, the Leadwing Coachman, Devil Bugs, and even Woolly Worms used on the surface are good. This represents a wide spectrum of patterns, I realize, but if presented in the proper areas or in the rise, all will produce satisfactory results.

Wet Flies, Streamers, and Bucktails

Wet Flies, Streamers, and Bucktails in Streams

In Maine, early season fly fishing is devoted for the most part to the use of streamers, bucktails and wet flies, in that order of popularity. Where landlocked salmon are concerned, the streamer is king, followed respectively by the bucktail and the wet fly. Where brook trout are dominant, the bucktail usually takes the lead, followed by the streamer and the wet fly. This is not a rule with every fly fisherman, but holds true over much of the state. The successful and tactful caster utilizes whatever he feels is necessary for results, regardless of what the rest of the clan is using, which is the way it should be in all aspects of fly angling.

Of these three, I prefer the small bucktail (size 8-12), tied to imitate vital fodder fish such as the dace, smelt, and shiner. This is particularly effective in streams and rivers, where currents offer assistance in disguising the pattern, and where movement of the water imparts pulsations to the bucktail hair.

Streamers, with their feathers, are excellent producers without question. Generally, however, these designs do not possess the natural freedom of the bucktail, primarily due to the over-dressing of comercially tied flies. Thinly constructed casting streamers, however, are deadly tools when used correctly and at proper times. Utilization of different patterns is a matter of personal preference in most cases, but the prepared fly fisherman should always carry a few selected patterns in each design.

Wet flies involve essentially the same story. While I do not utilize them a great deal, they are extremely productive when fish are feeding below the surface on larval life and dead insects. I have had my best results with wet patterns in the slower areas with a slow retrieve, while bucktails and streamers produce best in the faster whitewater stretches.

Experience has taught me that wet flies produce more fluently and consistently during the spring once water temperatures have warmed to a minimum of 50°. Trout in particular are actively feeding below the surface then (50° to 60° is ideal), and small (number 12 and 14) wet flies are highly productive. The color pattern of a wet fly, however, seems to make a difference at specific times of year.

Natural insects emerge in a succession of color shades. The darker-colored nymphal stages appear first—brown, black, blue, and gray—making imitations such as the Black Gnat, Dark Hendrickson, March Brown, and Iron Blue Dun and similarly colored wet patterns the best producers.

As spring wears, however, lighter naturals replace the darker nymphs, and such patterns as the Light Cahill, Light Hendrickson, White Moth, Gordon, and Professor begin to attract fish and are generally the best producers throughout the summer. Some dark/light patterns are good selections as well.

Some good all-season wet flies include the Blue Quill, the Hornburg, the Woolly Worm, and the Hare's Ear. A good general rule to remember: match the natural if at all possible; if darker nymphs or insect life are visible, utilize a dark wet fly, and follow suit with light colored naturals as well.

Unlike streamer and bucktail patterns, wet flies are best fished upstream in a dead drift. Remember, small wet fly designs imitate dead insects or certain naturals still in their nymphal stage—drifting naturally, but slowly, with the current. Cast up and across stream, allowing the offering to drift past holding areas and lies. Because the wet fly should be used most often in the slower current areas, drag should not present too much of a problem. Mending of the line will remedy the situation where drag restricts the freedom of the fly, however.

An important technique to remember when utilizing wet patterns is to keep the offering in the water as long as possible. I've had good results by casting in a quartering fashion upstream, allowing the dead drift, then working the fly gently against the current for five to ten feet once it has reached its zenith downstream. I then allow the fly to drift back several feet before casting upstream again. This gives the fly extra "working" time and offers a more natural appearance which often arouses fish curiosity.

Many of the popular Maine salmon rivers, the productive ones at least, maintain good smelt fisheries. This is the prime reason why streamer patterns such as the Gray Ghost, which utilize color combinations of white, gray, and black are favorite landlocked salmon flies. Where smelt runs are not heavy, other forage fish such as the shiner and dace will most likely be found, and in such areas, a number of other streamer flies and bucktails will produce results. Some of the more productive and popular streamers and bucktails will be mentioned in Chapter 5, "FEATHERED FRIENDS."

Realizing that the smelt is the landlocked's most cherished forage, however, is a great asset for the stream and river fisherman. Smelts usually start to enter or move up important tributary waters right after ice-out in Maine when the winter run-off is still high. Used with a sinking line, streamer flies are highly productive in the rapid and riffle areas at that time, and will continue to produce until the smelt run is over, or until the season's first hatch appears.

Brook trout, on the other hand, are not as selective as salmon, and will readily gorge themselves on any small, non-spiny fish. For this reason, bucktails and streamers are highly productive for stream and river squaretails during the early season and when surface insects are not available. As with streamer flies, there are many productive bucktail patterns (see Chapter 5, "FEATHERED FRIENDS"). But yellow, brown, black, white, red, orange, and green, or combinations thereof, are generally seen on more patterns than other shades, particularly when in the company of silver or gold worked tinsel bodies.

Tactically, bucktails and streamer flies are worked in a downstream fashion. Some fishermen utilize them upstream, but they are in the minority in Maine. The best method is to cast either directly downstream for 30 to 35 feet, or towards one of the banks, letting the fly drift with the current until it mends. It should then be worked with short jerks upstream past prospective lies.

As with the wet fly, keep these patterns in the water as long as possible. Retrieve your offering for 20 to 25 feet only, letting it drift back downstream with the current before allowing it to sit in a "dead" position for a half-minute or so. Then work the fly back upstream in the same fashion. If no action is received, cast again in a quartering fashion downstream (remember you only have to cast 30 to 35 feet) and try the tactic one more time. If action is still not found, change patterns, frequently to a smaller size.

A popular tactic of mine, particularly on the West Branch of the Penobscot and other rivers which offer a combination of fast and moderate flowing current, is the "panic strip". The cast is made, quartering upstream, allowing the current to carry the fly downstream past a possible lie. It is then retrieved upstream to a point where the fly is just below the holding area, and is suddenly stripped in rapidly, giving the appearance of a bait fish fleeing in panic after spotting the fish. This is often productive when fish do not seem to be biting in fast-water areas.

The idea behind using streamer flies and bucktails is to fish them deep in fast-water stretches where trout and salmon often congregate during the spring. It often helps to utilize weighted flies, particularly where currents have a tendency to keep the fly close to the surface.

In many "fly fishing only" waters, however, weighted flies are not allowed. We must then treat our leaders so they'll sink faster. Or use this tactic—submerge the tip of your rod so that it is just off the bottom, thus keeping line, leader, the fly down where the fish are.

Wet Flies, Streamers and Bucktails in Ponds and Lakes

Utilizing below-the-surface flies in lakes and ponds is quite different from the same used in streams and rivers. This is true for two principal reasons: first, fish inhabiting these larger areas are free to move about in search of food and may be found in any number of locations, depending upon the time of year. The second reason concerns the amount of natural forage available on the bottom of the pond or lake.

Extremely rich bodies of water, for example, warm rapidly after ice-out and seldom give their inhabitants reason for going to the surface. Cool water temperatures and sufficient food supplies close to the bottom are all a trout needs to be happy; in these cases, dry flies take few fish throughout the season. The majority of trout and salmon waters in Maine, however, do not fall into this category. Therefore, knowing what fish are feeding on and where to work your offering at specific times of the season is highly important. Working a fly which resembles the natural bait, and getting the offering to sink rapidly and with little disturbance, are also important factors.

There are basically two times of the season when wet flies, bucktails, and streamers are either necessary or helpful in taking fish: early spring before naturals start to appear, and during hot weather after dominant hatches cease and fish seek cooler temperatures in deep water. These two periods make up a large percentage of the fishing season over much of the state.

All important natural bait fish in Maine, such as the smelt, shiner, and dace genuses, are spring or early summer spawners. Those inhabiting lakes and ponds move into the shallow inlets and tributaries seeking gravel beds in which to mate, and are followed by trout and salmon. While these two predators may not actually enter smaller inlets, they will congregate near the mouths of these tributaries, awaiting the upstream movement of the smaller fish.

The use of small and medium casting streamers and bucktails (sizes 4 through 8) will produce results in these areas starting right after ice-out and for at least a month thereafter. By then, however, the majority of fly fishermen have reverted to floating imitations, particularly in the smaller ponds, since the latter part of most dace or smelt runs and the first emergence of naturals often occur simultaneously.

During warm weather periods, the streamer or bucktail angler should anchor boat or canoe approximately 100 feet from an outlet, casting his offering in towards the riffle areas. It is not necessary to put the fly into the whitewater, but what I call "strategic casting" is often productive.

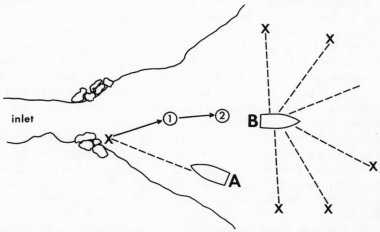

This diagram shows two productive techniques with below-the-surface flies off tributary mouths in the spring. In A, anchor to one side, and cast either upstream or on a quartering angle. Allow the fly to drift naturally with the current to points 1 and 2. In B, anchor in midstream and cast to spots beside and in front of your. This is deadly, especially for larger trout and salmon.

Select a position which will allow you to place the fly upstream of a possible lie or holding area. It may often be necessary to present on a quartering angle, but this will have to be determined on the spot. Allow the offering to roll down with the current, bringing it to life as it mends into the pond. This gives the appearance of a bait fish in trouble, and is often enticing to trout and salmon lying off the mouths of tributaries.

Do not offer the fly too much action once it has reached open water, however; you'll be defeating your purpose. A little nudge now and then, letting it "fall" downstream periodically, will do it.

Another productive tactic at this time, but only from a mid-stream position, is to cast as far as possible out into the pond or lake. Allow time for the pattern to get to the bottom, then retrieve with fast stripping of the line. At it nears the boat, change the action to a slower pace but continue with sharp jerks. This change in action and pace is often the deciding factor with fish who have been following the lure for any distance.

Try this technique at least three or four times in the same direction, always allowing sufficient time for the fly to reach the bottom. If no strike is received, try casting several yards to your left three or four times and continue to "fan" the entire area to the side and in front of you. Some of the larger and more skittish fish lie in deeper water further off the inlets, but can be enticed to the hook in this fashion.

Once the "bait fish" runs are over, and during times when surface activity is slow, streamers, bucktails, and particularly wet flies are productive on windward shores. Forage fish travel lakes and ponds in schools close to shore most of the time, at least until surface temperatures become excessively warm. Also, insects and terrestrial matter are pushed in that direction by the wind, and trout and salmon follow; wet flies should be fished with no control from the line, and streamers and bucktails should be worked slowly in around submerged boulders, rocks, and overhanging trees.

During the spring, fishing is most productive with sinking imitations before daybreak. This is principally due to the fact that most forage fish move into tributary waters after dark, continuing through the night, and also that salmon and trout feed predominantly before the sun hits the water. Once the morning is well underway and action in tributary areas starts to dwindle, working a well-shaded cove scattered with rocks and boulders may show some excellent fish as well.

Streamers and bucktails are often productive at the tail end of the fishing season in Maine. Again, spots near major tributary mouths are cooperative locations as salmon and trout move upstream or into the mouths, awaiting high water for their annual spawning migrations. Fish these areas in the same fashion as described earlier, particularly for landlocked salmon. Action may be found as early as the latter part of August, although the month of September is best.

In most cases, a sinking line is best for all aspects of below-the-surface fishing, or a floating line with a sinking tip may be recommended. When fishing lakes and ponds, however, many experienced anglers utilize a floating line, preferring to treat their extra-long *leaders* to sink rapidly. They reason that the floating line allows them to see when the fly is being accepted, and is easier to retrieve in fast water. I can agree with the latter belief, but the former is debatable.

In rivers and streams, again, line selection is a personal choice, although experience has taught me that a floating line with a sinking tip is best. However, choice has a lot to do with current water conditions and the type of water to be fished.

If the current is strong and powerful, for example, such as on some of the stretches on the Rapid River and West Branch of the Penobscot, I utilize a dry line with a "fast" sinking tip and treat my leader as well; this is also true when fishing deep in lakes and ponds. On the other hand, if the stream or river is shallow with a moderate flow, such as certain stretches of the Carrabassett and Sandy Rivers, a floating line with a treated leader may be all that is necessary. If I had to recommend one line to cover all below-the-surface fishing tactics and conditions, however, it would be a floating line with a "slow-sinking" tip. With this line, an angler can govern fly depth with his casts, drift, and treatment of the leader.

Nymphing
A Selected Tactic for a Selected Fraternity

Although I find it hard to swallow, being a dry fly fisherman at heart, more and bigger fish will be taken on the properly presented nymph than on any other type of artificial. The nymph is a deadly tool in all types of river and stream habitat as well as in lakes and ponds, and is readily accepted by landlocked salmon and trout inhabiting Maine waters.

But unlike other conventional wet patterns and dry flies, the nymph is the most unpopular and least-used tool of Maine fly fishermen. This is true for several reasons, but is primarily due to the difficult methods under which the nymph must be used to produce fish. With many experienced fly fishermen, however, it is also true simply because the nymph is not needed for productivity.

Burrowing May fly nymph (2X). Sketch
by Malcolm Redmond.

For all practical purposes, the nymph and the techniques with which it is
used are the study, and sometimes the passion, of a special fraternity of fly
fishermen. There are some who utilize nothing but these nymphal imitations
from ice-out to the end of the season with great success, finding that nymphing
is the only aspect of the sport which offers them any real challenge. These
anglers are rare in Maine, however, and the majority of nymph fishermen here
would fall under the "occasional use" category, offering them only at specific
times of year when the other wet and dry designs produce little action.

Purists in this fraternity will argue the point that, like dry flies, nymph
imitations should precisely match naturals. They will also insist that
quartering upstream is the best method in which to present them under most
circumstances. The first is debatable, but the second is basically true. Each
river or stream should be studied carefully before wetting a line, however, as
should the color and size of any visible insect. Knowing the size and coloration
of any resident natural, and understanding the current flow and depth of the
water, the angler can then go to work and present his offering accordingly.

Selecting Artificial Nymphs

When selecting artificial nymph patterns, it should be remembered that there are three natural insects of predominant importance which hatch on Maine waters; these are the May fly, the caddis fly, and the stone fly, respectively. Of these species, the May fly and caddis fly are most important, since the stone fly emerges for only a short period over much of the state and is largely overpowered by its two front-runners. Coloration of nymph patterns, therefore, should be similar to that of adult May flies and caddis flies. Size should vary between 10 and 16 for most patterns, although an occasional size 8 may be required in lakes and large rivers.

It is amazing how realistic artificial nymphs have become within the past few years. The use of latex, monocord, and other modern materials has given these patterns a likeness never before possible, and the selection of patterns by inexperienced fishermen is getting to be as complex and confusing as choosing productive dry flies. This indeed is unfortunate, for all the angler really has to do is select a number of patterns, in the sizes suggested earlier, in a variety of natural colors, including brown, gray, cream, olive, and black. To assist the novice in selecting his offerings, however, the following list of nymphs is suggested for use on Maine waters:

Black Nymph (also tied in brown, gray, cream, olive and yellow)
Atherton Dark
Atherton Light
March Brown
Leadwinged Coachman
Trueblood's Caddis
Light Cahill
March Brown
Gray Fox
Iron Blue
Hendrickson (Light and Dark)
Quill Gordon
Hare's Ear
Atherton Medium
Blue Wing Olive
Caddis Larvae (tied in colors of cream, green, olive and gray)
Zug Bug
Muskrat Nymph

Nymphs in Rivers and Streams

The idea behind nymph fishing is to put the offerings at the proper depth where fish can see them and accept them with the minimum amount of effort. Because of varying water temperatures and flow, trout and salmon will be found at different depths at different times of the year. If success is to be expected, the angler must know where and at what depth fish will be lying and present the nymph accordingly. Utilizing these offerings *at the proper level* can not be overemphasized. When action is not received with nymph patterns, chances are the offering is simply not at the proper depth.

In the early part of the season, fish inhabiting streams and rivers are found close to the bottom. They have eaten little during the winter months due to a slowing of their metabolism, but now, as warm water revives their mobility, they start to gorge themselves on available nymph life on the bottom. The angler should use a sinking-tip line at this time, and should cast quartering upstream to visible lies and holding areas. It may be necessary to treat your leader for fast sinking ability, and/or to use weighted nymphs which will drag along the bottom.

An important technique is to fish the nymph slowly into holding positions right under your quarry's nose. Remember—his metabolism is not up to par, and he will not travel a great distance for food. Access line should be stripped out to prevent drag, and when the offering has reached its zenith downstream, it should be left there for several minutes, given periodic twitches with the rod. Proper depth, and working the nymph into holding areas, are the keys to success at this time of year.

Once water levels have receded and temperatures have warmed, however, tactics with the nymph change slightly. Fish are now closer to the surface, accepting nymphal and insect life in the surface film. Nymphs become highly productive close to the surface, although during extreme hot weather, trout and salmon will be found close to spring holes and small feeder streams. The angler should keep this in mind and work the nymph accordingly.

Again, casting directly upstream or in a quartering upstream fashion is the best tactic. A floating line can be used at this time, and is the most popular with warm-weather nymph fishermen. In all cases, the rod should be kept fairly high with no drag on the line or fly; consistent stripping of the line is often necessary. To offer your pattern a more natural drift, a long leader (at least nine feet) is recommended; a 5X tippet also works very well in most instances.

The strike, or acceptance, on a nymph is usually very gentle. Fish often simply pick the offering up and start to swim off at a slow pace—if they do not reject it first. The angler, therefore, must develop an ability to set the hook at precisely the right moment. It is a difficult aspect of this art— watch the line, since the fly is below the surface, and learn to set the hook gently. Time and practice will be needed to develop this skill. But once mastered, a whole new world will be opened to the fly fisherman who formerly relied on wet flies, bucktails, and small casting streamers for early season and warm weather success.

Nymphs in Lakes and Ponds

Working the nymph in lakes and ponds is a productive tactic, particularly when surface activity is nil, or when streamers and bucktails have shown no action. Basically, the angler should keep an eye on the windward shore and on tributary mouths, and utilize a sinking fly line and long leader treated to sink rapidly. Scrape the offering along the bottom slowly during the spring, switching to a floating fly line and fishing the pattern close to the surface as the water warms on windy days.

Photo by Al Raychard

Chapter 4
TROLLING STREAMER FLIES

One of the most productive methods of challenging the cold water sportsfish inhabiting Maine's large lakes and ponds is the trolling of tandem-hooked streamer flies, or long-shanked streamers tied to resemble favorite fodder fish. The trolling of such flies is rich in Maine angling lore, highly productive at certain times of year, and an aspect of fly fishing which is gaining popularity throughout Maine. During the spring of the year (until water temperatures drive trout and salmon to cooler depths), and again in September, there is no method of angling as thrilling as trolling feathered or bucktail streamer flies in waters housing landlocked salmon, brook trout, or brown trout.

The streamer fly itself has been a popular angling tool in Maine since the turn of this century. Names such as Carrie Stevens, Herb Welch, Ai Ballou, Bill Edson, J. Herbert Sanborn, and Joseph Stickney have contributed such immortal patterns as the Gray Ghost, Black Ghost, Nine-Three, Supervisor, Ballou Special, Warden's Worry, and the Light and Dark Edson Tigers. But only since the early 1930s have such designs been commonly tied in the tandem-hooked style.

57

Originally, these and other patterns were tied for casting. But with the arrival of the outboard motor era, fishermen found that great success could be achieved by trolling them at a moderate speed through areas of characteristic salmon and trout habitat. The problem of short-striking fish soon became a dilemma, however. And if it had not been for this fact, perhaps we would never have seen the tandem-hooked adaptation.

Two Maine natives are given credit for conceiving this double-hooked trolling fly—J. Herbert Sanborn and Emile Letourneau. Both men are known for their many contributions to the impressive list of Maine-oriented streamer designs. But considering that the trolling of such patterns is one of the most popular tactics on Maine lakes and ponds today, the development of the tandem streamer is perhaps Sanborn's and Letourneau's greatest contribution to the angling fraternity.

The use of double-hooked streamers has become an accepted way of life in Maine. On lakes such as Sebago, Rangeley, Moosehead, and East Grand, where landlocked salmon and trout populations are impressive, the trolling fly is without question the most popular tool utilized in the search for action. And it would not be unrealistic to estimate that nearly 75 percent of the salmon and brook trout taken from these four major lakes are taken on either tandem or long-shanked streamer flies. Their use and popularity is widespread on other Maine lakes and ponds as well—wherever landlocked salmon, brook trout, and brown trout are found.

As with dry and wet flies, there are numerous streamer patterns available. The majority of the more productive designs are tied with bucktail, feathers, and tinsel to resemble important fodder fish, particularly smelt and shiners. But attractor patterns such as the Mickey Finn, Royal Coachman, and Tri-Color are extremely productive as well. Designs imitating natural feed are more popular with fishermen and produce more action than attractor types, but only because of their heavy usage.

There are three basic factors which determine whether a salmon or trout will strike at a passing streamer fly. The most important factor is curiosity, followed by jealousy, then greed. And I have found this to be true with common wet and dry fly and nymph as well.

If a fish is curious about an object, or if it attracts his attention, he will surely investigate, which explains why salmon and trout often follow a fly for a considerable distance before striking. Therefore, the drawing power of a streamer or any underwater fly is highly important to the fisherman. Experiments have shown that the coloration of a streamer, and utilizing the proper color variations or combinations at specific times or under certain conditions, are greater keys to success than actually imitating a smelt or another single forage fish.

The eyesight of fish, as most anglers know, is extremely keen—contrary to belief, they are not color blind. I am a firm believer that certain colors, particularly orange and red, can be seen at greater distances by fish than can most other shades, but only to certain depths. This explains why the Mickey Finn is one of the best shallow trolling streamers or casting streamers the fly fisherman can utilize.

On many of Maine's clear lakes, the light of the sun on a bright day will penetrate to a depth of only about 30 to 40 feet, and, on rainy or overcast days, to a lesser degree. On bright days, patterns tied with bright colors such as orange, red, and yellow, and possessing tinsel bodies, produce better at depths of up to 40 feet. On overcast days, or when it is necessary to troll in deep water, streamers constructed of darker materials in shades of blue, green, and purple will outfish the brighter patterns two to one.

For this reason, I do not necessarily buy a streamer just because it imitates a smelt, perch, or shiner. In most cases, and on the majority of Maine lakes, action will be found if the fisherman utilizes nothing but attractor patterns—*if* he considers the lighting, knows the general depth of the fish and whether or not the fish are in a biting mood, and uses the properly colored fly at the proper depth.

Personally, my favorite streamers are attractor types, although I carry a wide variety of color combinations in bright, light, and dark shades for use at specific times. Deceiver-type streamers have always been more popular with Maine fishermen, and unquestionably will produce fish, but I think that their success depends upon the skill of the individual fisherman, and that their importance has been over-emphasized.

The dedicated lake fisherman often makes as much of his chosen sport as the dry fly or nymph fisherman makes of his. It is, without question, a skill and an art to masterfully take landlocked salmon, brook trout, or browns in a large body of water. The lake fisherman must know the likes and dislikes of his adversary when it comes to water temperature and preferred feed, and must know how to present his offering in such a manner that it appears as natural and attractive as possible. He must also know where trout and salmon will be at given times of the year, and how to use a streamer capable of enticing the fish to the hook.

It is quite common for the streamer enthusiast to carry numerous designs in both attractor and natural imitation patterns. When the tandem-hooked streamer was first contrived, however, the familiar casting streamer patterns were converted to the double-hook design—and it is these patterns which continue to be the selected choices of trolling fishermen year after year.

Such patterns include the Gray Ghost, Black Ghost, Nine-Three, Supervisor, Barnes Special, Spencer Bay Special, Liggett's Special, Golden

Witch, and Jane Craig. These streamers are renowned throughout Maine for their productive characteristics on salmon. But they are equally attractive with large brook trout and browns inhabiting lakes as well.

There are, however, other designs which have achieved recognition with Maine fishermen through the years. And including them in one's fly box often proves an asset, particularly when fish appear to be selective and action calls for experimentation with different color combinations. This list includes the Red Gray Ghost, Green Ghost, Mickey Finn, Colonel Bates, the Dark and Light Edson Tigers, Grand Lake Special, Pink Lady, Lady Ghost, Royal Coachman, Yellow Perch, Parson Tom, and Winnepesaukee Smelt.

Buying these and other tandem-hooked streamer flies is not a difficult job. It should be remembered that the favorite producers resemble fodder fish and are usually tied in grays, whites, shades of brown, black, and green, or combinations of these with lighter colors. But it should also be remembered that most of the flies displayed in the tackle shop are gaudy misconceptions on behalf of the professional fly tier, as are 90 percent of the artificials bought by the fishing public. It is not, however, the fly tier's fault—*our own* misconceived notion that a sparsely tied fly is cheap, unproductive, and not worth the money we pay for it has led to this state of affairs.

In fact, the *best* streamers are those sparsely tied, and I have also found that it makes no difference whether or not the pattern is equipped with eyes. This need for eyes on a streamer is also a misconception—it is indeed unfortunate that novice trolling fishermen are told otherwise, and thus refuse to utilize a streamer unless it pleases their eyes, and has a pair of its own as well.

One of my favorite trolling flies is a tattered and badly-haired Miss Sheron, which has taken more than its share of salmon from Sebago and Richardson Lakes. To the eye, it appears worthless, supporting just about a dozen pieces of deer hair. But to me it is worth the price of several new streamers, for it produces action when "better-looking" flies fail.

When a new streamer is purchased, I often take it aside and, with a pair of scissors or pliers, strip it of heavy or lengthy hair and feathers. And if the eyes appear over-sized or unnatural, it is very likely that they will disappear as well. It is of little importance to me how a streamer, or any fly for that matter, appeals to my eyes. It *is* important, however, that the coloration is right, and that the body, wing, and hackle are in proportion to the hook (the sparser the better). The only exception involves selecting dry flies when trying to match a specific natural insect, or when the need arises for a high-floating pattern in rough water; it is then when thick, stiff hackle is a necessity for appearance's sake.

There are several ways to utilize the trolling streamer. But because I am a student from the waters of Sebago Lake, I have been taught a particular technique which I have respectfully labeled the "Libby Method."

Arthur Libby of Standish has been a registered Maine guide, and a guide on Sebago Lake, for more than three decades. He started fishing the lake as a boy in 1927, and through the years his knowledge and skill at trolling streamer flies has given him a reputation such as few modern day Sebago guides enjoy. From his creativity have come such popular trolling patterns as Miss Sheron, Green Wonder, A.W.L., Senator Muskie, Rain, Songo Smelt, and Libby's Cal, all of which are unsurpassed for taking landlocked salmon on Sebago Lake. Only the old standbys such as the Gray Ghost, Nine-Three, Black Ghost, Mickey Finn, and perhaps Supervisor, take more fish, or are more popular, than the Libby flies. This is only because they have been around longer and have had more publicity.

In 1953, Libby conceived a technique for trolling streamer flies which has proven productive for me not only on Sebago, but on Rangeley, Moosehead, Mooselookmeguntic, Richardson, and wherever I have used it in seeking salmon. By trolling the proper flies in the proper areas, however, this technique is equally deadly on brook trout and browns as well. And I believe it to be the best method in which to troll tandem, or long-shanked, streamer flies.

This method requires an eight- or nine-foot rod, to which is attached a six-inch extension on the butt. This acts as a brace, or rest, for the rod when fighting salmon, and has shown itself to be highly important when battling large, powerful fish.

A large reel is also needed—and one of the best is the Pflueger SAL-TROUT. About 30 yards of black nylon backing is installed first, followed by a level number 6 sinking (L6S) fly line. Libby insists that this be a green line in a 50-yard length. Finding a *green* fly line is not that difficult, but as far as I know, Scientific Angler manufactures the only 50-yard fly line, and it can be hard to locate.

I have, therefore, been experimenting for the fast few seasons with a *standard* length number 6 sinking line, and I quite honestly have found it to be no less cooperative. There are times when all the fly line and some of the backing is let out to set my fly down a few more inches. But under most circumstances, a standard length fly line will work most pleasingly.

It is the leader used in this method, however, which most often surprises folks—a 45-foot, eight-pound test, piece of camouflaged monofilament is required. Libby says you can use this leader until it is down to 35 feet long, but then must replace it. As in most forms of fly fishing, the longer the leader, the better the fly acts and looks in the water. Through experimentation, I have learned that this lengthy leader which the "Libby Method" calls for is, without a doubt, the single most important tool governing success of the streamer fisherman—other than the streamer itself.

Trolling a streamer is an art and a skill which takes time to master. When salmon and trout are biting, it seems that any pattern, trolled in any pattern, trolled at any depth, will provide action. But it is when fish are uncooperative and the angler still finds productivity that really proves the skill and determines the caliber of the fisherman. Knowing where fish will be at certain times, and knowing how to entice them to the flies, determines a fisherman's skill—not necessarily the number of salmon or trout he brings home.

Streamers are most productive when salmon are close to the surface—when water temperature varies between 40 and 60 degrees. However, several old-time guides I know and respect believe that salmon will rise close to the surface, within 20 feet or so, at least once every 24 hours to feed. During the warmer months, this will generally take place in areas where cold water can be reached in a hurry or is readily available. This is a good point to remember, particularly in July and August.

As with live bait, the streamer fly is most productive if trolled at a certain speed, and if more than one fly is being used in a certain fashion. Art Libby once told me the best trolling speed for streamer flies is "at a fast walking pace," or three to four miles an hour. "The way I tell," he'd say, "is by looking at the trees on the shore, and I judge my speed in comparison to their movement. If that don't work, I speed up to where I think is right and continue to accelerate until I get action."

Along with speed, placement of the flies has proven an important factor as well. I find it more productive to stagger my gear, with the two outside lines reaching further back than the two inside lines. No two flies are trolled at the same distance, however, and the outside lines are nearly always rigged with attractor flies such as Miss Sheron, Mickey Finn, or Red and White, while the inner two carry imitative patterns, their coloration depending upon time of year and depth of the fish.

As a rule, the streamer fly is a surface lure, most often used in depths varying from 10 to 30 feet. This is characteristically the favored depth of landlocked salmon and brown trout in large bodies of water. But the brook trout is often found in deep water, and as water temperatures rise, salmon and brown trout will seek the cooler temperatures of deep water as well. It is often required, therefore, to go down with the streamer to get any action.

To do so, and to stick to fly fishing tactics, we must add weight to our line—or change lines completely, utilizing a sinking fly line with a lead core.

Such lines have been manufactured for years by Gladding, but may be difficult to find in certain areas.

The easiest way to get the streamer down to where it can do its job is to add a 10-yard length of lead core line between the leader and the regular fly line. There are fishermen who splice the lead core between the backing and the fly line, but I think they are defeating their own purpose. This set-up is trolled at a slightly slower speed, which also gets the fly down to the right depth, but as a rule, the regular trolling speed needed to entice salmon can be maintained.

The single most important fodder fish of the Maine landlocked salmon is the smelt. Characteristically, these silvery members of the family *Osmeridae* are deep swimmers, traveling in schools off tributary rivers and streams, rocky shoals, dropoffs, and rocky bars. Basically, wherever smelt will be found, salmon will be found to some degree as well. The smelt is also a favorite dish of brown trout, brook trout, and lake trout—and even largemouth and smallmouth bass will devour them whenever they have the opportunity.

It should be remembered, then, that the most productive time of year for trolling streamer flies is when smelt are moving into tributary rivers and streams on their annual spawning runs, bringing the landlocked salmon into this shallow water with them. Although the actual date of migration upstream varies in different areas of the state, the fisherman can generally expect movement by mid-May. The streamer fly, worked at a fast trolling speed in shallow water off known smelt running rivers, is deadliest during these runs. And a knowledge of seasonal smelt migrations on popular salmon and trout lakes is a fisherman's key to success.

Generally speaking, once the smelt run has started, action with streamer flies will continue to be extremely productive for three to four weeks, and the fisherman can expect to be in his glory until warmer water temperatures drive the salmon to cooler depths. At that time, action will slow somewhat, but some of the best fish are taken as the smelt runs start to fade. Continued faith and work in a certain area will often produce more results than will continuous movement about the lake looking for action.

As the season wears and September approaches, streamer flies again become highly productive as salmon start to move into major tributary waters on their annual spawning runs. While action is not usually as high then as during the spring smelt migrations, a late August or early September rain which increases the flow of water will often start salmon moving upstream early, bringing action for the fisherman.

Characteristically, landlocked salmon spawn from early October to the end of November, but this varies according to locale and current water conditions. A late summer rain will often draw mature adults to tributary mouths, although they may not actually enter or spawn for several weeks.

Trolling close to these tributaries can be highly rewarding, considering that spawning landlocked salmon in Maine are usually between the ages of three and six. Depending upon water chemistry and other factors, such fish may vary between 16 and 23 inches and weigh over the four-pound mark. Some of the finest salmon taken by streamer flies annually are those taken near the mouths of major spawning tributaries in late August and September.

While the majority of streamer fishermen in Maine are primarily after landlocked salmon, the brown trout is highly susceptible to the tandem or long-shanked trolling fly as well. And this *Salmo trutta* has become a popular target in habitats where salmon or brook trout cannot exist.

Like the salmon, the brown trout accepts a streamer with a violent attack, often followed by a long, powerful run. Once the hook has been set and the fish has tasted steel, instinct tells him to escape and the fisherman has a magnificent battle on his hands! The lake-bred brown is an impressive and powerful jumper, even more than his stream inhabiting brother—he will often fight and resist right to the net.

Pound for pound, however, the brown does not have the fighting power, or the long-lasting trait of almost tirelessly challenging the fisherman, possessed by the salmon. He often tires quickly when the hook is set deep and the leader allows some persuasion from the angler. But when resisting, or if the fisherman is weary of mastering his prey, the brown is truly a fighting and challenging dynamo who will test the skill of the most experienced streamer fisherman, particularly if the fish has some weight and girth on his side. It is this fighting spirit and unique intelligence, along with his willingness to accept trolled streamer flies when salmon are resting in cooler depths, that has made the brown the second most sought-after game fish of trolling streamer fishermen over much of Maine.

While salmon and brook trout seem to prefer trolling flies which resemble forage fish, the brown is not quite so particular in lakes and ponds. *Salmo trutta* is often considered the most wary and selective trout in Maine rivers and streams, but experience has shown me that this is not always the case in deep lakes when trolling flies are used.

Patterns tied tandem, or single-hooked patterns on a #2 or #4 8x long-shank hook covered with bucktail or feathers in shades of brown, black, and white, or brown and white, are highly productive, particularly just before sunrise and just before and during those last remaining minutes after sunset. I have had good luck on streamers tied with a mixture of yellow and brown topped with a touch of white, but this combination does not seem to work effectively on *all* brown trout waters.

In waters where landlocked salmon and brown trout share the habitat, browns are often found in areas characteristic of salmon, but will not go as deep as water temperatures grow warmer. In such lakes, trolling deceiver flies such as the Gray Ghost, Supervisor, Nine-Three, and Black Ghost, just as you would for salmon, will produce browns even in July and August; early morning and late afternoon just before dark provides the best action. Becaust of this, a good selection of attractor and deceiver flies is recommended. In most cases, I have found, when trolling for brown trout, that streamers made of bucktail, whether of the attractor or deceiver fashion, produce better than those tied of feathers.

Without question, the four most popular salmon and trout lakes in Maine where streamer flies are avidly used—perhaps even considered vital for success—are Sebago, Rangeley, Moosehead, and West Grand. It is these renowned waters which draw the bulk of streamer fishermen each year, both resident and non-resident. Somehow, it would not seem fit to write a chapter on trolling streamer flies without mentioning these famed and highly productive habitats.

SEBAGO LAKE

Because it is given credit as the original home of the landlocked salmon, Sebago is perhaps the best known salmon lake in Maine. It was here where the world's record landlocked salmon was creeled in 1907. And although it was

East Sebago, Sebago Lake

Photo by Carroll Cutting

not taken on a streamer fly, it is nevertheless a distinction to have a Maine lake listed in the world angling books.

Sebago has seen the birth of several nationally accepted streamer flies, the most famous being the Barnes Special. Besides the patterns mentioned earlier, conceived by Art Libby, such patterns as the Lady Ghost, Arnold, and Green Ghost were derived from experimentation on Sebago both before and after the arrival of the outboard motor. These and other trolling patterns are highly popular, and streamer flies continue to take more landlocked salmon from Sebago each season than any other type of lure.

Generally speaking, salmon fishing with streamer flies starts to get hot at Sebago right after ice-out. The date of open water varies from year to year, but one can usually expect portions of the lake to be fishable by early or mid-April. At that time, salmon are congregating close to the mouths of major tributaries such as the Songo, Panther, and Muddy rivers, in anticipation of the smelt run which may or may not have already taken place. At any rate, the waters off these and other tributary mouths are the fisherman's best bet for success.

During the months of May and June, Sebago is at its best for the streamer fisherman. Salmon have, for the past couple of years, been more willing to cooperate, and because of the location of smelt and suitable water temperature, fish are not overly difficult to locate. Action is usually productive, with excellent salmon, some weighing in the five-pound class, being seen quite regularly.

As recently as six years ago, it was difficult for the best salmon fisherman to net an example weighing a pound-and-a-half. Today, however, Sebago has returned to the point where it can consistently produce acceptable specimens running anywhere from three to four pounds, with an occasional five- or six-pounder thrown in just to keep the angling fraternity's attention. I predict that Sebago will continue to prosper, again producing the caliber salmon for which it was famous worldwide only two decades ago.

During the early months of spring (May and June), salmon can be found close to shore, enjoying the easy availability of the smelt and the cool, comfortable water temperatures. At this time, your attractor patterns are extremely productive, and will continue to be so until warmer water drives the fish down—usually by the first of July on Sebago. After this time, darker-colored flies will produce more results at these greater depths.

The use of streamer flies usually slows dramatically in July and August on Sebago. But at times, the lake will experience a week-long flurry when salmon will be found close to the surface and will readily accept flies. This is not necessarily an annual event, and whether or not the "August flurry" appears depends upon water temperatures and movements of the smelt population.

September is usually a productive month at Sebago, and is a time which devoted streamer enthusiasts anxiously await. While water temperatures may still be fairly warm close to the surface, spawning can draw mature adults close to the major river mouths by the first week of September, and action can be excellent then. Exceptionally active areas are just off the mouths of the Songo, Muddy, Northwest, and Panther rivers.

Personal experience has taught me that September is a time for the attractor fly at Sebago. Generally speaking, this is the case on many of Maine's landlocked salmon lakes. While imitative streamers are also productive at this time, the fact that salmon eat little during the spawning run tells me to rely on their curiosity to make them strike. Along with this, the fact that they are usually lying in relatively shallow water tells me again to use brightly decorated and colored streamers on bright, sunny days and duller, or darker-colored, flies on overcast or rainy days. While this is not an absolute rule, I have found it helpful over much of the state.

RANGELEY LAKE

Of the various lake systems in Maine, none have contributed as much to the streamer fly fraternity as the Rangeley Lakes; the number of patterns which

Rangeley Lake

Photo by Maine Dept. of Commerce and Industry

have been born in these waters is indeed impressive, outnumbering any other lake system in the state. Most have stood the tests of time and continue to be popular with the modern streamer fisherman, taking trout and salmon throughout the world.

Originally, Rangeley Lake itself was known for its magnificent brook trout fishery. It is said that this town and areas surrounding it were born not from farming or lumbering, but from rich city businessmen journeying there from around the globe to fish for native brook trout. This is most probably true, and Rangeley and surrounding towns such as Oquossoc and Hain's Landing continue to offer guiding services and sporting camp accommodations which can be matched by none other than perhaps those on Moosehead Lake.

By the mid-1800s, however, the wear and tear on Rangeley's native trout population was taking its toll, and by 1875, landlocked salmon were introduced; they have been an important resource throughout the Rangeley system ever since. In the early 1900s, the landlocked became the predominant fishery. And in Rangeley, Mooselookmeguntic, and the Richardson lakes, they are still the most sought-after game fish by far.

The use of streamer flies on Rangeley Lake continues to be popular today. Ironically, however, hardware lures such as the Mooselook Wobbler are challenging the streamer as the most utilized trolling tool. Fishing styles have changed in this region since 20 years ago, when trolling streamers were unquestionably the selected choice of salmon and trout fishermen. Still, during the spring and fall fishing seasons, tandem trolling flies will outfish metal lures, keeping the tactic alive in an area which has been synonymous with streamer flies since 1902 when Herb Welch tied the first pattern at Oquossoc.

Because of Rangeley's high altitude and severe winter conditions, ice-out comes later than on southern Maine waters. The date has been as early as May 2, but Rangeley has held ice until May 27 as well. As a rule, however, the lake will be free of ice sometime between May 15 and May 18, and trolling will be possible, although conditions may not be perfect.

Rangeley houses some fine, healthy salmon, but since 1975, the lake's smelt population has been declining, thus affecting the salmon fishery. To put it simply, there is not enough feed to support the present salmon population. This undoubtedly will change when present biological studies are completed, and there is no question that Rangeley will produce salmon in the three- and four-pound class regularly, recovering from its depression the way Sebago did.

There are two primary productive periods when Rangeley is at its best for catching landlocked salmon: in the spring, during the two or three weeks immediately following ice-out, and in the fall, during the last two or three weeks of September. While salmon can be, and are, often taken throughout the open season, the highest catch ratio occurs during these two periods.

In the spring, Hunter Cove is usually the first place where action is received. But early action is also available off Rangeley Lake State Park, in and off the points of Greenvale Cove, and near South Bog and Dickson's Islands; these are also the prime areas in September, particularly Dickson's Island and Greenvale Cove.

Large brook trout are uncommon sights in Rangeley Lake today. But every now and then, an impressive example is taken, usually on hardware lures close to the bottom. Streamers trolled close to shore during the spring will take brook trout from Greenvale Cove, and some are seen around the islands. But for the remainder of the season, squaretails are too deep for the streamer fisherman, unless he wishes to sink his fly to the bottom for them.

The majority of streamer flies originating from the Rangeley area were composed of feathered wings and tinsel bodies—it is these deceiver flies which are still the favorite choice of Rangeley fishermen. Attractor patterns are not very popular, although I have taken salmon on the Mickey Finn and the Warden's Worry. Bucktail streamers are popular to a certain degree, but the following patterns are sold more than any others at Dick Frost's Rangeley Region Sports Shop: Gray Ghost, Black Ghost, Pink Lady, Supervisor, Nine-Three, and Barnes Special.

The Blue Smelt is a popular pattern, as is the Warden's Worry—the Parmachene Belle is the most avidly bought attractor. Number 4 tandem-hooked streamers are preferred over the long-shanked designs.

MOOSEHEAD LAKE

Moosehead is Maine's largest lake. Like Sebago and Rangeley, it has an impressive angling history, and enjoys the prestige of being Maine's most popular fishing retreat. Much of the fame which surrounds the Moosehead region derives from the fact that this inland sea is capable of producing some magnificent brook trout, as well as landlocked salmon. But it is the mystical attractions, along with the angling fame, which make Moosehead one of the biggest tourist centers in the Northeast.

The air is fresh, the waters are crystal clear, and the surrounding woodlands abound with wildlife. From Greenville, it is possible to head due north by boat and dock 40 miles away at the small villages of Northeast Carry or Seboomook. At Moosehead is available the greatest collection of sporting camps and seaplane services, and the largest assemblage of registered Maine guides, in the state, all catering to the visiting fisherman and sportsman.

East Outlet Dam, Moosehead Lake

The streamer fly is a popular spring and fall trolling tool on Moosehead. Salmon and brook trout are taken regularly with tandem patterns, and those imitating forage fish are without a doubt more popular than attractor types; long-shanked trolling streamers are utilized as well, but are not as popular as the tandem.

The spring fishing season on Moosehead starts with ice-out, generally about the 15th of May. Depending upon weather conditions, however, open water may be available a week earlier or later, and action is favorable with surface streamers for about three to four weeks. During this time, both landlocked salmon and brook trout are taken frequently, although each species appears to restrict itself to specific locations throughout the lake.

On the west shore of Moosehead, there are two productive areas for salmon during the spring and fall seasons: off the Moose River to a point about halfway to Kineo Island, and along the west shore, from Socatean Cove south to Rockwood Point. The Moose River itself is highly productive also, as is the area off Hardscrabble Point on Kineo.

Brook trout action during May and September can be found off Socatean Stream, and squaretails can generally be taken during these times off the larger streams and brooks entering the lake. Two prime examples are Tomhegan Stream and Baker Brook, both north of the town of Rockwood.

On the eastern shore, the situation is pretty much the same, with the majority of success each spring and fall occurring off major tributary waters and around the many islands dotting the coves.

Landlocked salmon are sought off Black Point near Lily Bay State Park, and off Birch Point outside of Beaver Cove. The Narrows between the state park and Sugar Island is often a productive area, particularly in May. And the area off the Roach River in Spencer Bay is cooperative during both the spring and fall seasons.

From Greenville north along the eastern shoreline, there are numerous islands, and I have found the shoals in these areas to be productive, especially in May and early June when salmon are still close to the surface. Two of my favorite spots are the waters around Salmon Island off the mouth of the Roach River, and around the Moody Islands south of Kineo Island. These areas are not deep, averaging between 25 and 54 feet, making them ideal spring salmon grounds.

I have had little luck with brook trout along the east shore. But a stray will be taken on occasion with streamers off the points, shoals, and tributaries north of the state park. Moosehead houses some of the best brook trout to be found in Maine's large, deep lakes but, because of its great expanse, they are sometimes difficult to find.

As mentioned earlier, streamer flies tied to resemble forage fish are the preferred choice of most Moosehead fishermen. The Gray Ghost is one of the most popular patterns, along with the Pink Lady, Nine-Three, Supervisor, and Black Nose Dace, all tied tandem. The most common size streamer is a number 6.

WEST GRAND LAKE

West Grand Lake has become recognized in recent years as one of Maine's most productive landlocked salmon waters. Located in Washington County, it was one of the original homes of the Maine landlocked, although it never quite reached the pinnacle or received the attention given to Sebago. This is indeed unfortunate, for West Grand has all the characteristics, and houses sufficient resources, to satisfy even the purest of streamer fishermen.

The area surrounding West Grand is a secluded region. As a result, the lake, its people, and its salmon fishery have been able to hold on to the charisma that other areas such as Sebago, Rangeley, and even Moosehead lost when we entered the mobile age. The countryside is truly scenic, the people are friendly, and the fishing, whether in the lake itself or in Grand Lake Stream, is among the best remaining in the state for landlocked salmon.

Grand Lake Stream

Photo by Dave O'Connor

Surprisingly, West Grand Lake experiences an early ice-out, and open water fishing generally starts by the last week of April or the first week in May. Conditions may not be perfect this early, but action is often productive. The size and weight of West Grand salmon vary, as in other habitats, but some excellent examples hitting the three- and four-pound mark are definitely in residence there.

Like many landlocked salmon waters in Maine, West Grand is a fairly deep lake, 128 feet at its deepest; the average depth is right around the 50-foot mark. There are numerous shoals, rocky points, dropoffs, and islands which create some ideal habitat for landlocked salmon, and productivity is well diversified over much of the lake. Action is often consistent throughout the summer, even in July and August when other salmon waters may be slow. May, early June, and September are the prime angling periods, however.

In the spring, the trolling streamer fisherman will find action from Kitchen Cove Point south along the east shore to the dam at Grand Lake Stream. Chances for success and productivity are often good from Big Mayberry Cove, located on the west shore of the lower bay area, south to the dam. The reefs and dropoffs around Munson Island are good salmon areas, too. These same locations are prime fall trolling locations.

The Narrows between the main lake and Junior Bay is one of the most popular trolling areas on West Grand, and the islands within Junior Bay itself, particularly around Bear Island, produce some fine salmon throughout the season. Pocumus Bay is a hot landlocked area from ice-out through September as well.

Predominantly, there are seven popular streamer fly patterns utilized at West Grand Lake. Number 4 or 6 long-shanked hooks are unquestionably the choice there, and it is rare when a tandem streamer is seen.

Heading the list of favorites are two local flies, seldom seen in other areas of the state: the Golden Head and the Grand Laker. These two patterns are utilized more, and take more salmon, than any other streamer. The Gray Ghost is popular here, as are the Nine-Three, Pink Lady, Supervisor, and Ranger.

I have taken the space to cover Sebago, Rangeley, Moosehead, and West Grand lakes in depth primarily because these four waters are the most popular landlocked salmon and streamer fly areas in the state. There are, however, numerous other salmon waters which produce excellent action annually, and the following generalized list contains some of my favorites.

No effort has been made to establish prime fishing dates or productive locations on these waters. It is recommended, if more detailed data and information is required, that the angler patronize a local fly or tackle shop in that area or contact the local Chamber of Commerce. (addresses can be found in appendix).

Photo by Dave O'Connor

OTHER GOOD TROLLING SPOTS

LAKE	TOWN/COUNTY	PRINCIPAL FISHERY
Ossipee Lake	Waterboro/York	LL Salmon/Brown Trout
Great East Lake	Acton/York	LL Salmon/Brown Trout
Hancock Pond	Sebago/Cumberland	Brown Trout (This is one of the best brown trout waters in Maine)
Long Lake	Bridgton/Cumberland	LL Salmon
Moose Pond	Bridgton/Cumberland	LL Salmon
Aziscohos Lake	Lincoln/Oxford	LL Salmon/Brook Trout
Parmachenee Lake	Lynchtown/Oxford	LL Salmon/Brook Trout
Upper/Lower Richardson Lakes	Richardsontown/Oxford	LL Salmon/Brook Trout
Umbagog Lake	Magalloway Plt/Oxford	LL Salmon/Brook Trout
Mooselookmeguntic Lake	Richardsontown/Oxford	LL Salmon/Brook Trout
Kennebago Lake	Davis Twp.	Ll Salmon/Brook Trout
Dodge Pond	Rangeley	LL Salmon
Spencer Lake	Hobbstown/Somerset	LL Salmon/Brook Trout
Lake Moxie	The Forks/Somerset	LL Salmon/Brook Trout
Attean Lake	Attean Twp./Somerset	LL Salmon/Brook Trout
Big Wood Lake	Jackman/Somerset	LL Salmon/Brook Trout
Brassua Lake	T. 1, R. 1/Somerset	LL Salmon/Brook Trout
Chesuncook Lake	T. 3, R. 11/Piscataquis	LL Salmon/Brook Trout
Chamberlain Lake	T. 6, R. 11./Piscataquis	LL Salmon/Brook Trout
Lobster Lake	T. 3, R. 14/Piscataquis	LL Salmon/Brook Trout
First Roach Pond	Frenchtown/Piscataquis	LL Salmon/Brook Trout
Sebec Lake	Willimantic & Dover-Foxcroft/Piscataquis	LL Salmon
Scraggly Lake	T. 7, R. 8/Penobscot	LL Salmon/Brook Trout
Grand Lake Matagamon	T. 7, R. 8/Penobscot	LL Salmon/Brook Trout
Cold Stream Pond	Enfield/Penobscot	LL Salmon
Eagle Lake	Wallagrass/Aroostook	LL Salmon/Brook Trout
Square Lake	T. 15, R. 5/Aroostook	LL Salmon/Brook Trout
Portage Lake	Portage Lake/Aroostook	LL Salmon/Brook Trout
Fish River Lake	T. 13, R. 8/Aroostook	LL Salmon/Brook Trout
East Grand Lake	Danforth/Washington	LL Salmon
Big Lake	Indian Twp./Washington	LL Salmon
Damariscotta Lake	Nobleboro/Lincoln	LL Salmon

EASTERN
STREAMERS

Photo by Jack Hawthorne

Chapter 5
FEATHERED FRIENDS

One of the most important chores of the productive fly fisherman is the selection of flies. Whether they are wet, dry, streamer, nymph, or bucktail type, the imitations we carry afield very often determine our success. Presentation, proper drift, and action, both on top and below the surface, govern a trout's or salmon's interest. But experienced and successful fly fishermen know it is the fly on the end of the tippet which draws the strike.

Before the actual purchase or selection of imitations can be made, however, certain factors must be understood. This is particularly true here in Maine, where fly fishing tactics and entomological conditions are quite unorthodox when compared with other areas of the country, or even other parts of New England. It should always be remembered, especially when fishing the waters of this state, that while proper fly selection is highly important, successful anglers are often those who take their time and work a pool or riffle area slowly and in proper fashion.

On remote trout ponds, and even while trolling streamer flies, the productive fisherman knows where his quarry is likely to be lying at certain times of year. He knows where the spring holes are, or which dropoffs are apt to hold fish, and he works his offerings accordingly.

In the case of the seasoned streamer fisherman, the selection of his pattern is often ritualistic. He chooses a favorite design which, over the years, has been productive at that time of year. This is also the case with many dry fly and wet fly enthusiasts, who use their favorites except perhaps during a specific hatch when the natural is preferably matched with an artificial. That, however, is the case for only a short period during the Maine season.

As in most famed salmon and trout regions, there are basically three insect genuses of importance to the Maine fly fisherman. They are, respectively, the May fly, the caddis fly, and the stone fly. While the May fly is the most important of the three, the caddis fly has, in recent years, become increasingly dominant in certain areas of the state.

Wet, nymph, and floating imitations of the caddis fly have risen to new heights of popularity within the past decade, and are extremely productive on Maine waters at appropriate times. This is particularly true in the Rangeley Lakes region, which has one of the largest caddis emergences in the state.

The May fly, however, continues to be the most influential insect in the Maine fly fishing arena. Members of the order *Ephemeroptera* are found in well-established numbers throughout the state, although emergences on many southern waters have lessened noticeably within the past decade.

Slightly warmer water temperatures and pollution are two determining factors. And there is a good chance that the caddis will become the primary forage insect in southern Maine as conditions worsen. This does not mean, however, that the May fly is gone from southern waters and that May fly imitations no longer produce there. Quite the contrary.

In northern and western areas of the state, the May fly situation remains healthy. Being on a remote pond or standing knee-deep in a productive stream during a dominant May fly hatch can be described as nothing less than fantastic. Not only do the fish become amazingly active on the surface, but the sky about you is literally clustered with adult flies preparing for the mating call. It is truly one of the most magnificent sights a dedicated fly fisherman can witness-and it is difficult to forget.

The May fly, unlike the caddis, has an incomplete life cycle by insect standards, transforming from the egg to the nymph stage and finally to the adult stage. Of these three stages, only two—the nymph and the adult—are of importance to the fly fisherman. And of these two, imitations representing the adult are most popular, although not necessarily the most productive for most of the season. These imitations representing the adult stage of the May fly are dry flies. Imitations representing the nymph stage would be nymph-type patterns, and certain small wet patterns.

Nymph imitations are extremely productive on Maine waters. Because of the delicate skill needed to work them properly, however, they are utilized by only a few skilled anglers and purists. The majority of fly fishermen in Maine rely on small wet patterns instead of nymphs, primarily because they are easier to use, yet still produce results. As the season progresses, the dry fly gradually replaces the wet fly, and the nymph is generally ignored by the vast segment of the fishing fraternity.

For those who know how to utilize the nymph in its proper fashion, however, more productivity will be found under more circumstances than with any other fly design. This is true in the spring before adult naturals have emerged, throughout the season when hatches are sporadic, and at the tail end of the season when the large hatches have ceased.

While the list of May fly nymph patterns is impressive, I have learned that those tied in sizes 12 through 16 are most productive in natural shades of cream, green, gray, olive, and light brown. Larger nymph patterns in sizes 8 and 10 are often necessary on some of the larger rivers such as the West Branch of the Penobscot and sections of the Saco and Kennebec. But on most of Maine's trout and salmon rivers, particularly the Rapid, Kennebago, upper Magalloway, and Crooked, the smaller sizes are all that is necessary.

Below is a list of popular May fly nymph imitations:

Atherton Light
Atherton Medium
Atherton Dark
March Brown
Hendrickson
Gray Nymph
Quill Gordon
Dun Variant
Light Cahill
Iron Blue

(Regional nymphs are also very popular. Check with local fly shops).

From about the first week of June throughout the open season, the dry imitation representing the adult May fly is the most popular design statewide. Only after the caddis fly has emerged does the dry May fly imitation decline in popularity. But the standard May fly designs are the best known and most used. This is true even during stone fly hatches, which are considerably less dramatic than those of the May fly and caddis.

Adult burrowing May fly (life size).
Sketch by Malcolm Redmond.

It should be understood that once the May fly has reached its adult stage, it undergoes two changes which are of great importance to the dry fly fisherman; these are the *dun*, when the May fly first emerges from the water, and the *spinner*, which occurs after the actual mating has been completed and the May fly lies spent on the water. There are dry imitations tied to resemble each segment of life. The regular dry fly represents the dun and the spent-wing design imitates the spinner. Both fashions should be carried by the angler.

If the fisherman had to choose between the two, however, he would be better off to select the regular dry fly, since trout and salmon are more inclined to rise to the *subimago* (dun) as it dries its wings than to the *imago*, or spinner.

As with nymph imitations, the list of dry May fly patterns is impressively long, often confusing to the novice or inexperienced fly fisherman, and completely unnecessary for productive fishing in Maine. The careful selection of a dozen or so dry flies in a variety of sizes from 10 to 16 will produce results under almost any circumstances. Here's why.

Unlike the streams and rivers of New York, Vermont, and Pennsylvania, the waterways in Maine are comparatively poor in insect life. Although we experience fair hatches of insects, they are much smaller, and last for a shorter period of time, than those in states containing waterways with high algae, alkaline, or acid content, which are capable of supporting larger amounts of nymph and larvae life per acre.

Because of this fact, our trout and salmon are slightly less selective than in other parts of the East. You might say they are willing to accept what they can get when they can get it, as long as the presentation, drift, and appearance are somewhere near right. Nevertheless, because the rivers, streams, and ponds throughout much of the state are amazingly clear and often shallow, enticing these prized specimens to the hook is still a challenging and often perplexing pastime.

The majority of May fly genuses emerge during the late afternoon or early evening hours in Maine, usually after water temperatures have reached 53 degrees or higher; from approximately 1:30 p.m. to 6:00 p.m. are vulnerable hours, with the height of most emergences seen at about 4:00 p.m. Most hatches continue until after dark, with a few stragglers still present the next morning; (very few, however, and these more common on ponds than on streams and rivers).

As a rule, May fly hatches start to occur in southern Maine as early as the first week of May, but only on a small scale and depending a great deal upon the weather. By the third week of May, however, emergences are underway in that section of the state south of a line running in a convex path from the town of Bethel to Waterville and up along the coast to Eastport. This varies according to existing conditions. Dominant hatches in the south cease by mid-June. North of this imaginary line, emergences take place starting between Memorial Day and during the first week of June, and stretch into early July with sporadic appearances thereafter.

Dry fly fishing is highly productive during these hatches, and knowing that the quarry is not overly selective is a great asset. Instead of trying to match *Stenonema vicarium* precisely with a March Brown or Great Red Spinner, or *Stenonema fuscum* with a Gray Fox, I try instead to match the emerging natural with an imitation of the same size and comparatively the same color or shade combination.

For example, if a creamish or grayish natural is emerging and is roughly a size 14, I would offer a Light Cahill or Adams in the same size. If a darker fly was appearing, perhaps a Quill Gordon would be used; if the natural happened to be lighter, a Gray Fox or Hendrickson may be tied on; etc.

What I am saying is: it is not absolutely necessary to carry an exact twin for each May fly that emerges on Maine waters, but it is important to match the natural in size and coloration whenever possible. With that in mind, the following list of dry flies is recommended:

Adams (sizes 12-18)
Quill Gordon (sizes 12-18)
Hendrickson (sizes 12-18)
Light Cahill (sizes 12-16)
Gray Fox (sizes 12-16)
Blue Wing Olive (sizes 14 and 16)
Whirling Blue Dun (sizes 14-18)
March Brown (sizes 12-16)
Red Quill (sizes 12-16)
Gordon (sizes 14-18)
Iron Blue Dun (sizes 12-16)
Dark Cahill (sizes 12-16)
(all patterns listed here in size 10 are excellent for rough water)

When the large hatches of May flies start to taper off, the caddis fly appears in all its glory and spendor, keeping trout and salmon active close to the surface. The transition from May fly dominance to caddis dominance is rapid in many areas, as if *Trichoptera* couldn't wait to burst into life. Caddis flies and May flies often appear simultaneously during this changeover period. But after the first Saturday of July, the caddis is generally the dominant insect.

Again, because of weather and water conditions, appearance in southern areas may be seen earlier or later than this date, perhaps as early as the last week in June in extreme northern regions, perhaps as late as mid-July elsewhere.

I have three favorite dry fly designs to imitate the adult caddis. But I have learned there are many floating patterns which work equally well. As with the May fly floaters, I prefer natural color combinations of brown, green, gray, olive, tan, and black, usually in sizes 12 through 16. Since the majority of my fishing during the "caddis season" is on rivers for landlocked salmon, slightly larger-than-usual floaters are preferred. In extreme rough areas, size 10 flies are readily used.

I particularly like the Hairwing Caddis in sizes 12 and 14. It is a good basic design and can be tied with hackle in a variety of colors; it is especially effective in the quieter riffle areas when floated high on long drifts.

The Gray Caddis is another favorite. Several years ago, I experimented with this down-wing pattern, tying it in a number of color combinations, and it worked extremely well in the Rangeley area. Larger examples of this pattern work well in the riffle and rapid areas of the West Branch. But it is equally as productive on the Kennebago and Rapid Rivers.

A third favorite is the Grasshopper. With its feathered down-wings over the body, it bears a superb resemblance to a caddis resting on the surface. This, in size 10 and 12, is an excellent choice for rough water stretches. But smaller Grasshoppers in sizes 14 and 16 will produce in quieter areas as well.

Again, this pattern is best if tied in shades of brown and green. However, the body of this fly tied in yellow and orange is popular with many fly fishermen; when it is used to imitate the caddis, I have found little use for the red hackle barbules on the tail.

One of the most productive dry fly patterns during a caddis hatch in Maine is the Wulff. Small black, gray, and white Wulffs are extremely productive in rivers with rough current when a natural of the same color is emerging; the Coachman Wulff is highly effective just before dark.

There are, of course, a host of other dry flies which produce results during a caddis emergence. Some are intended to specifically imitate the caddis, some are not. But all have proven to be excellent selections. These include:

Sedge Fly (sizes 10-12)
Brown Sedge (sizes 10-14)
Dark Brown Sedge (sizes 10-14)
Green Sedge (sizes 10-14)
Gray Wulff (sizes 10-12)
Henryville Special (sizes 12-16)
Humpy (sizes 10-16)
Montana Wulff (sizes 10-12)

(Do not hesitate to use popular May fly patterns during a caddis fly hatch; they often prove highly effective. Popular examples include the Adams size 12, Hendrickson size 12 and Light and Dark Cahills sizes 10-12.)

The caddis fly experiences a complete insect life cycle, going through a larval state to pupa, adult, and adult female ovipositing stages. Unlike the May fly and stone fly, the caddis mates more than once, often up to three times, and has a life expectancy of up to 20 days. This is another reason why the caddis is slowly becoming more populated over much of the state.

Even though it has a complete life cycle, the only stage of life of importance to the Maine fly fisherman other than the adult is the pupa, or nymphal, stage.

Adult caddis fly (2X). Sketch by Malcolm
Redmond.

But here again, because of the skill required to work the caddis nymph
properly, it is not overly popular with the majority of fishermen. Nevertheless,
to assist those who do utilize the caddis nymph, the following list of popular
and productive larva and nymph patterns is suggested:

**Green Caddis Larva (sizes 8-16, also good in cream, olive, and
gray)**
Dark Caddis Pupa (sizes 8-14)
Jorgensen Caddis Pupa (sizes 8-14 in gray, tan, and olive)
Solomon's Caddis Pupa (sizes 8-14 in gray, tan, and olive)
Gray Caddis Pupa (sizes 12-18)

The stone fly is the last noticeably important trout and salmon insect with which the fly fisherman should be concerned. It is far less important than the May fly and caddis, but anglers should be familiar with this insect and carry several dry imitations which resemble the genus *Plecoptera*.

Like the May fly, the stone fly has an incomplete life cycle; only the nymph and adult stages are of importance to the fly fisherman. However, because the stone fly often emerges while the caddis adult is still in command, little attention is given to the stone fly nymph over much of the state. Popular stone fly nymph artificials include:

Bird's Stone Fly Nymph No. 2 (sizes 4-10)
Giant Black Stone Fly Nymph (sizes 2-10)
Surette's Brown Latex Stone Fly Nymph (sizes 2-10)
Little Green Latex Stone Fly (sizes 12-16)
Early Stone Fly (sizes 12-14)
Montana Stone (sizes 8-12)
Truebloods Stone Fly Nymph (sizes 8-12)

Adult stone fly (life size). Sketch by Malcolm Redmond.

Characteristically, the stone fly is an early emerger over much of its domain. But in Maine waters, it follows the caddis, usually appearing no later than late June unless adverse weather and water conditions dictate otherwise. It is quite common to see both caddis flies and stone flies over a given water at the same time; on many waters with rich bottoms, these two insects are even joined with sporadic appearances of May flies as well.

The stone flies which hatch in Maine are large specimens, much larger than most genuses of May fly and caddis. Because of this, and because fast and moderate streams and riffle areas are prime emerging sites, large artificials work extremely well; at least size 12 is suggested, and size 10 is popular.

Unlike the May fly and caddis, there are few good imitations representing the adult stone fly, particularly for this part of the country. Patterns in yellow, dark brown, olive, tan, and black, tied in a down-wing fashion and supporting a lot of hackle, work best. Two popular commercial patterns, however, are the Early Brown Stone Fly and the Light Stone Fly. Although most fly tying books suggest that these two designs be constructed in sizes 12 or 14, try them on a number 10 hook; they work extremely well on fast water such as the Rapid River and stretches of the Penobscot River.

The Golden Stone in sizes 12 and 14, the Sofa Pillow in sizes 8 through 12, and the Little Yellow Stone in sizes 10 through 14, are also excellent artificial patterns.

When these three important insect genuses have lost their effectiveness over much of the state, salmon and trout start to accept other artificial imitations. If we were to check fly boxes, we would find that the productive fly fisherman carries a host of non-imitative patterns which have proven effective through the years on Maine waters.

While May fly, caddis fly, and stone fly imitations will take fish most of the time, even when the insects are not present, the following dry flies are recommended and are highly productive on Maine ponds, rivers, and streams:

Black Gnat (sizes 10-18)
Fan Wing Royal Coachman (sizes 10-14)
Mosquito (sizes 12-16, size 10 for rough water)
**Hornberg (sizes 10-14, this is also an excellent pattern fished
        wet sizes 6-10)**
**Muddler (sizes 10-14, excellent in rough water and a good
        wet pattern in sizes 6-10)**
Black Ant (sizes 12-18)
Green Drake (sizess 8-12)
Cream Variant (sizes 12-14)
Irresistible (sizes 10-16)

Female Beaverkill (sizes 12-16)
Brown Bivisible (sizes 1-16)
Royal Coachman (sizes 10-16)
McGinty Bee (sizes 10-14)
White Moth (sizes 10-18)
Badger Spider (sizes 12-18)
Green Leafhopper (sizes 18-20)
Black Midge (sizes 18-22)
Gold-Ribbed Hare's Ear (sizes 12-16)

Small wet flies are highly productive patterns on Maine waters, particularly during the early spring in streams and rivers. Those designs carrying the same name as the more popular dry imitations are usually more cooperative. But some of the attractor and non-imitative patterns are productive as well:

Quill Gordon (sizes 12-14)
Pale Evening Dun (sizes 12-16)
March Brown (sizes 8-12)
Light Cahill (sizes 12-16)
Dark Cahill (sizes 12-14)
Gold-Ribbed Hare's Ear (sizes 10-16)
Dark Hendrickson (sizes 12-14)
Coachman (sizes 8-16)
Black Gnat (sizes 8-12)
Montreal (sizes 8-14)

The bucktail and casting streamer are synonymous with fly fishing in Maine. They are highly popular during the early season when fishing streams and rivers for landlocked salmon, but are productive with brook trout as well. They are best utilized with a sinking line, close to the bottom in rapid areas, or where riffles empty into deep pools.

Initially, these two patterns were designed to represent forage fish such as the smelt, shiner, and dace. They were tied with natural color combinations ranging from white and gray to green, and right on down the line to black. The Gray Ghost, Black Ghost, and Nine-Three are perfect examples.

As time passed, however, and as more was learned about how light and water clarity effects a trout's or salmon's response to a below-the-surface fly, it was discovered that some bright-colored flies composed of bucktail produced excellent results. This was particularly true on Maine's clear, rapid streams and rivers which were exposed to high light densities. The Mickey Finn had always been a favorite and productive fly, and other such attractor patterns were soon to follow.

As a rule, I would rather utilize an attractor casting bucktail than a imitative streamer. But this is not a rule; I am just fond of the bucktail design, whether it be an "attractor" type, or one such as the Black Nose Dace. I feel that they offer better action in the water, particularly in fast water. And because of this action, they have more drawing power to the hook.

I do not mean to denounce the feathered streamer, however. Such patterns work wonders when fish are feeding on smelts and shiners in the spring, especially in rivers and large streams. Such designs are best tied sparsely (which also applies to the bucktail); they produce best on cloudy days and/or in deep pools. The bucktail attractor is best used on bright days or in clear rivers and streams. And the bucktail imitative designs produce well in ponds, all types of rivers, and streams where comparative forage fish exist.

Below is a list of popular and productive feathered streamer flies and bucktails:

Black Ghost (sizes 8-12)
Black Marabou (sizes 6-12)
Black Nose Dace (sizes 6-12)
Gray Ghost (sizes 6-12)
Marabou patterns in yellow and white (sizes 6-12)
Mickey Finn (sizes 8-12)
Supervisor (sizes 6-10)
Barne's Special (sizes 6-10)
Colonel Bates (sizes 6-10)
Light Edson Tiger (sizes 6-10)
Dark Edson Tiger (sizes 6-10)
Green Ghost (sizes 6-10)
Nine-Three (sizes 6-10)
Parmachene Belle (sizes 6-10)
Red and White (sizes 6-10)
Royal Coachman (sizes 6-10)
Tri-Color (sizes 6-10)
Jane Craig (sizes 6-10)
Warden's Worry (sizes 6-10)
Golden With (sizes 6-10)

MAINE INSECT EMERGENCE DATES

(These dates are approximate and can vary considerably, affected by water and weather conditions).

ABOVE THE LINE:

May fly—May 30-June 26
Caddis fly—June 24-July 15
Stone fly—June 24-July 31

BELOW THE LINE:

May fly—May 5-June 17
Caddis fly—June 15-July 10
Stone fly—June 20-July 31

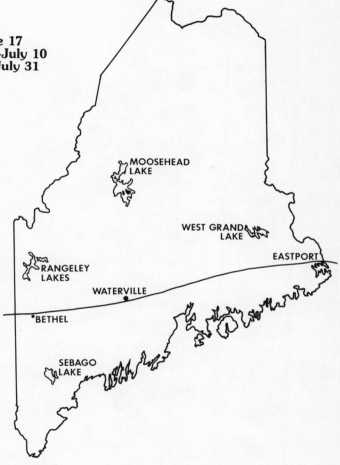

Photo by Maine Fish and Wildlife Dept.

Chapter 6
WHERE TO GO

One of the most important and difficult tasks in planning a Maine fly fishing trip is selecting the pond, river, or stream to fish. Considering the energy situation, it is important that we choose an area where we know trout will be found.

With this in mind, this chapter has been carefully compiled to supply basic information concerning some selected waters in each county of the state. The counties are arranged alphabetically, and the lakes within each county are likewise arranged alphabetically.

While this is not a complete listing of all trout and salmon waters in Maine, these waters have been either fished by me personally or recommended by registered Maine guides, float plane pilots, or fellow fly fishermen who were kind enough to supply information. The information which follows each water is updated and should help those anticipating or planning a trip to that water.

Waters within Baxter State Park are found in a special listing at the end of this section.

Included in the lake listings are recommended dates when production is normally best, and a list of flies which, under normal circumstances, should entice fish to the hook. These dates are "probable" active periods, and may vary considerably according to current weather, water, and insect conditions. The lists of productive flies, likewise, contain those which do not necessarily match the resident naturals, but which have been popular and productive on those waters. Keep in mind that action may be found at other times throughout the open season and with other offerings.

When I mention wet flies; I am referring in most cases not only to typical wet patterns, but to bucktails and streamers as well. This was done due to space restrictions.

While not always so, those waters with special notes saying "accessible by *vehicle* via" a certain gatehouse or the North Maine Woods, I suggest four-wheel drive. You may not always need it, but conditions in the remote country often change rapidly, and those planning to utilize the family automobile or standard two-wheel drive pick-up should contact resident Maine Forest Service personnel or the North Maine Woods for vehicle recommendations well in advance of their visit.

Remember as well that on the majority of the remote waters there are no state-maintained boat launching sites. Parties with larger boats and outboards should keep this in mind—the canoe and paddle is the most feasible craft in these areas, and often, it will be necessary to portage over a trail to reach the pond.

Included in this chapter are 10 "author's selected waters", which I highly recommend. Maps are included as well, indicating specific areas to fish during the spring, summer, and fall. These waters have been fished by me many times, and have become annual targets which I try to hit at least once each season. There are waters for the hiker, for the person who wishes to drive right to the pond, and for the wilderness enthusiast as well.

For the river and stream fisherman, I have included some of the best trout and salmon waterways I have found in my years as a Maine fly fisherman. Some are remote—others are reachable only by boat—still, the majority can be reached by automobile. Nymphs are often highly productive in these waters, and I have supplied the names of some nymphal and pupal imitations which are popular and effective here. But don't forget to experiment!

Fly size recommendations are intended to apply to all flies in each category: nymphs, wet flies, streamers, and dry flies.

Following the lake listings and maps is a short section dealing with a new resource in Maine—the salt water brown trout. Descriptions of the fish and his habits, methods of fishing for this sporty scrapper, and where he can be found—all are included, for I feel that the avid fly fisherman will enjoy tangling with these newcomers.

The following abbreviations and symbols are utilized in these listings: *—preceding the name of the water, this indicates that there are regulations on the water *other than the statewide general law*. All anglers planning a fishing trip in Maine should obtain, and read, a copy of the open water fishing laws before setting out on their jaunt; FFO—Fly Fishing Only; NLFAB—No Live Fish As Bait; BkT—Brook Trout; Bs—Bass; LL—Landlocked Salmon; BrT—Brown Trout. Mention of a species indicates the *principal* fishery.

These listings which are boxed are the "Author's Top Ten"—maps of these waters are included at the end of the lake listings.

AROOSTOOK COUNTY

*Black Ponds (Two Little), T15,R.9. FFO. BkT. Best times, late May through June; early July; September. Productive flies—dry: Mosquito, Adams, Light Cahill, Light Hendrickson, March Brown, orange-bodied Grasshopper, size 12. Within North Maine Woods, best reached through St. Francis Gatehouse.

Carr Pond, T.13,R.8. LL, BkT. Best times, mid-May through early July; September. Productive flies—wet: Mickey Finn, Gray Ghost, Black Ghost, Nine-Three, size 6-8; dry: Adams, Light Cahill, Light Hendrickson, Black Gnat, orange-bodied Grasshoppers, size 12. This is a good pond for trolling streamers for both salmon and trout. Salmon will come to the surface during a hatch. Best reached by air from Patten.

*Deboullie Pond, T.15,R.9. NLFAB. BkT. Best times, mid-May through June; evenings in July; September. Productive flies—wet: Mickey Finn, Black Nose Dace, Gray Ghost, size 6-8; dry: Gray Wulff, Mosquito, Dark Cahill, Black Gnat, size 10-14. A good trolling lake in early season. Located with the North Maine Woods, best reached through the St. Francis Gatehouse.

*Denny Pond, T.15,R.9. FFO. BkT. Best times, late May through June to mid-July; September, mornings and evenings. Productive flies—dry: Adams, Light Cahill, Light Hendrickson, March Brown, Mosquito, size 12-14. Located within the North Maine Woods, best reached through the St. Francis Gatehouse.

Farrar Pond, T.11,R.10. BkT. Best times, mid-May through early July. Productive flies—dry: Mosquito, Adams, Light Cahill, Light Hendrickson, Black Gnat, size 12. Located within the North Maine Woods. Reached through the Six Mile Gatehouse. Best reached by air from Patten.

*Fish River Lakes Region (Thoroughfares), T.13,R.8, T.14,R.8. NLFAB. LL. Best times, mid-May through mid-July, mornings and evenings; September. Productive flies—wet: Mickey Finn, Gray Ghost, Black Ghost, Nine-Three, Suprvisor, size 6-8; dry: Gray Wulff, Adams, Light Cahill, Light Hendrickson, March Brown, size 10-14. One of the best landlocked salmon areas in Maine. Use wet flies early; dry flies as water recedes and in the pools and riffle areas. Action will depend upon water level.

*Gallilee Pond, T.15,R.9. FFO. BkT. Best times, late May through June to mid-July. Productive flies—dry: Adams, Light Cahill, Light Hendrickson, Quill Gordon, Black Gnat, Mosquito, size 12-14. Located within the North Maine Woods, best reached through the St. Francis Gatehouse.

*Hudson Pond (Upper), T.11,R.10. FFO. BkT. Best times, late May through early July. Productive flies—dry: Mosquito, Adams, Light Cahill, March Brown, orange-bodied Grasshopper, size 12. Within the North Maine Woods, best reached through the Six Mile Gatehouse.

*Island Pond, T.15,R.9. FFO. BkT. Best times, late May through June to mid-July. Productive flies—dry: Adams, Mosquito, Light Cahill, Black Gnat, Quill Gordon, Gray Wulff, Light Hendrickson size 12-14. Within the North Maine Woods, best reached through the St. Francis Gatehouse.

*McKeen Lake, T.14,R.10. NLFAB. BkT. Best times, mid-May through late June; September. Productive flies—wet: Mickey Finn, Dark Edson Tiger, Black Nose Dace, Gray Ghost, Tri-Color, size 6-8; dry: Adams, Light Cahill, Light Hendrickson, Mosquito, Black Gnat, size 12. This is a good wet fly pond; troll with wet patterns behind the canoe with wet line. Located within the North Maine Woods. Best reached by air from Patten.

*North Pond, T.14,R.9. FFO. BkT. Best times, mid-May through June; early July evenings; September. Productive flies—dry: Mosquito, Adams, Light Cahill, Black Gnat, Light Hendrickson, size 12. Within the North Maine Woods, best reached through the St. Francis Gatehouse.

*Stink Pond, T.15,R.9. FFO. BkT. Best times, mid-May through June; early July evenings. Productive flies-dry: Mosquito, Adams, Light Cahill, Light Henderickson, Black Gnat, size 12-14. Located within the North Maine Woods, best reached through the St. Francis Gatehouse.

*Upper Pond, T.15,R.9. FFO. BkT. Best times, mid-May through June; July evenings. Productive flies—dry: Mosquito, Adams, Light Cahill, Light Hendrickson, Black Gnat, size 12-14. Located within the North Maine Woods, best reached through the St. Francis Gatehouse.

CUMBERLAND COUNTY

*Adams Pond, Bridgton. NLFAB, opens last Saturday in April. BkT. Best times, late May and June; September. Productive flies—it is not imperative to match the natural insect. The Mosquito, Black Gnat, and Grasshopper are good dries, size 10-14.

*Crooked River, Casco, etc. FFO. LL, BkT. Best times, for salmon, late August to end of season; for brook trout from early May through late June in upper stretches. Productive flies—for salmon: caddis and May fly nymph patterns in colors of light brown, olive, cream, and black, size 10-16. This is basically not a dry fly river for salmon. In September try small casting streamers imitating fodder fish. For brook trout: Mosquito, Hendrickson, Adams, and Wulff patterns in brown and gray are good, size 10-14. The Crooked has an excellent population of salmon but best chances are during the fall run—late August to September. Hit the rapid and deep pool areas. Brook trout are available throughout the season in the cooler stretches above Bolster's Mill in Otisfield. The river is narrow and congested in this area but offers excellent fishing.

Hancock Pond, Sebago. BrT. Best times, early May through June. Productive flies—in the spring, casting streamers at dusk and early in the morning are good. In June, small dry flies are best just before dusk. Try the Light Cahill, Hendrickson, and Adams, size 14. Action is slow but chances for appreciable fish are good.

Little Sebago, Windham. Bs. Best times, early May through June. Productive flies—Black Ghost, Red and White Bucktail, Nine-Three, Mickey Finn. Streamers are best used in the coves and off rocky points on this lake. Use a sinking line and dressed leader for best results.

Otter Pond, Standish. Bs. Best times, late May and June. Productive flies—small streamers cast near shore. Cannot be reached by automobile. This is a good place for children.

FRANKLIN COUNTY

*Arnold Pond, Coburn Gore. FFO. BkT. Best times, mid-May through June; dawn and dusk through season. Productive flies—wet: Muddler, Little Brook Trout, Light Cahill, Hendrickson, size 10-12; dry: Adams, Light Cahill, Hendrickson, Quill Gordon, Mosquito, size 12-14. Located close to Route 27. Receives a great deal of pressure but some good fish are available.

*Beaver Pond, Seven Ponds Twp. FFO. BkT. Best times, mid-May through the season. Productive flies—all May fly and caddis fly imitations in wet and dry patterns, size 12-14.

*Big Island Pond, Seven Ponds Twp. FFO. BkT. Best times, mid-May through mid-June. Productive flies—streamers: Gray Ghost, Black Ghost, Dark and Light Edson Tigers; dry: all May fly imitations, size 12-14. This is a large pond with large trout potential. Action is best during a natural emergence.

*Caribou Bog, Chain of Ponds. FFO. BkT. Best times, mid-May through June; dawn and dusk through season. Productive flies—this is a dry fly paradise! All floating May fly and caddis fly imitations in sizes 12-14.

*Carrabasset River, Carrabasset Valley. FFO. BkT. Best times, early June. Productive flies—brown, cream, olive, and black May fly and caddis fly style nymphs, size 12-16; dry: Adams, Light Cahill, Dark Hendrickson, Gray Fox, Gray Caddis, size 12-16. This is a very rapid stream in places but has some excellent deadwater areas. Must be worked slowly and carefully.

*Dead River, including North Branch and Alder Stream, Jim Pond, Alder Stream Twps. FFO. BkT. Best times, mid-May and June. Productive flies—dry: Adams, March Brown, Light Cahill, Light Hendrickson, Gray Wulff, Ginger Quill, Red Quill size 12-16. These rivers are highly productive trout waters. The North Branch is easily accessible from Route 27 and is heavily fished. Best results will be found away from the highway. Alder Stream is slightly smaller and hard fishing due to thick growth along the banks.

*Island Pond, Little, Seven Ponds Twp. FFO. BkT. Best times, mid-May through season, best at dawn and dusk. Productive flies—wet: Light Cahill, Ginger Quill, Dark Cahill, Dark Hendrickson; dry: Light Cahill, Dark Cahill, Dark Hendrickson, Mosquito, Adams, Black Gnat, size 12-14. This is a good, isolated trout pond, best fished at dawn or in the late afternoon and early evening during a hatch. Primitive camping close by.

*Jim Pond, Little, T.1,R.5. FFO. BkT. Best times, mid-May through season. Productive flies—wet: Light and Dark Hendricksons, Light Cahill, Quill Gordon, size 12; dry: Light and Dark Hendricksons, Light Cahill, Adams, Quill Gordon, Black Gnat, size 12-14; Hairwing Caddis, Gray Fox, size 10-16; streamers: Black Ghost, Blue

Smelt, Gray Ghost, size 6. Streamers are best early in the season. Wet patterns take over in early May until first emergences appear.

*Kennebago River, Lower Cupsuptic. FFO. LL, BkT. Best time, September. Productive flies—dry: Adams, Hare's Ear, green-bodied Grasshopper, Henryville, Gray Fox, Gray Wulff, size 12-16; wet: Gray Ghost, Black Ghost, Green Ghost, Blue Smelt, Supervisor, size 8-10. The Kennebago River is one of the best salmon and trout rivers in Maine. It offers excellent fishing for both species. Must be fished slowly and carefully, particularly in pools and eddy areas.

*Mountain Pond, Rangeley. FFO. BkT. Best times, mid-May through June at dawn and at dusk. Productive flies dry: Adams, Light Cahill, Brown Humpy, Yellow Humpy, Dark Cahill, size 12.

*Quimby Pond, Rangeley. FFO. BkT. Best times, May, June. Productive flies—wet: Black Ghost, Blue Smelt, size 6; dry: Black Wulff, Dark Cahill, Sedge Fly, Black Humpy, size 10. Quimby offers excellent trout and has a healthy caddis hatch each June, starting about the 15th.

*Rangeley River, Rangeley. FFO. LL, BkT. Best times, June-September. Productive flies—dry: Adams, Hare's Ear, green-bodied Grasshopper, Henryville, Gray Fox, Gray Wulff, Black Ant, size 12-16; wet: Gray Ghost, Black Ghost, Green Ghost, Blue Smelt, Supervisor, size 8-10.

*Round Mountain Pond, Alder Stream Twp. FFO. BkT. Best times, mid-May through early July. Productive flies—wet: Little Brook Trout, Light Edson Tiger, Dark Edson Tiger, size 6-10; dry: yellow-bodied Grasshopper, March Brown, Gray Fox, Yellow Humpy, Mosquito, size 10-14. Round Mountain Pond can be reached by the fishing public after a ¾ mile hike (over a steep ridge) but it is well worth the effort. Canoes are not available at pond. Pond wadable for some distance from shore due to gradual drop.

Sandy River, Phillips. BrT. Best times, mid-May through June in late afternoon and early evening. Productive flies—all caddis and May fly nymphs in brown, olive, gray, and black, size 12; dry: Hairwing Caddis, Gray Fox, Gray Caddis, March Brown, Adams, Light Cahill, Light Hendrickson, size 12-14. The Sandy River offers good fishing for brown trout. The water is clear and tactics must be conducted cautiously.

*Tim Pond, Tim Pond Twp. FFO. BkT. Best times, May, June, September. Productive flies—wet: Green Woolly Worm, Blue Smelt, Marabou, size 6; dry: Red and White Devil Bug, Green and White Devil Bug, Black Gnat, Iron Blue Dun, Hare's Ear, size 12-14. Tim Pond is one of the best trout ponds in this area. Time will be needed to get used to it but fine fish are possible. Action is heavy during a hatch over much of the pond in the evening and at dawn. Fish calm shore during a wind when using dry flies.

OXFORD COUNTY

*Abbie Pond, T.4,R.6 (Bowmantown). FFO. BkT. Best times, late May through June and throughout the season at dawn and dusk. Productive flies—Mosquito, Black Gnat, Adams, Hendrickson, Gray Wulff. Can be reached only by air—beautifully isolated.

*Aziscohos Pond, Magalloway. NLFAB. BkT. Best times, mid-May through June in the early evening and at dawn. Productive flies—wet: White Miller tied with red head. Little Brook Trout, Light Cahill, Iron Blue Dun; dry: Adams, Hendrickson, Quill Gordon, Mosquito, March Brown.

*Barker Pond, T.4,R.6 (Bowmantown). FFO. BkT. Best times, late May and June. Productive flies—Mosquito, Adams, Black Gnat, Hendrickson, Gray Wulff. Extremely remote, best reached by air.

*Beaver Ponds, Magalloway. FFO. BkT. Best times, mid-May through June. Productive flies—wet: Dark Hendrickson, Dark Cahill, Ginger Quill, Iron Blue Dun; dry: Dark Hendrickson, Whirling Blue Dun, Quill Gordon, Mosquito, Light Cahill, size 12-14. Some appreciable brook trout are available here. Caddis dry fly imitations are often good.

*Cupsuptic River, Lower Cupsuptic Twp. FFO. BkT. Best times, late May-early June. Productive flies—all caddis imitations in wet, dry, and nymph forms, sizes 12-14. The Cupsuptic is a small river with a combination of deep pools and riffle areas. Can be waded but caution should be taken; the water is crystal clear and the fish spook easily. Use fine-tipped leaders.

Garland Pond (Little Ellis Pond), Byron. NLFAB. BkT. Best time, May. Productive flies—dry: Black Ant, Grasshopper, size 12-14; streamers: Black Ghost and other fodder fish imitations, size 6.

*Howard Pond, Hanover. FFO and trolling only. LL, BkT. Best times, May; June; September. Productive flies—streamers: Blue Smelt, Red and White Bucktail, size 6.

*Magalloway River, Upper, Parmachenee Twp. FFO. LL, BkT. Best times, May and June for both species. Productive flies—for salmon: casting streamers such as the Gray Ghost, Black Ghost, and Mickey Finn. Dry flies for salmon include Adams, Quill Gordon, Hendrickson, Light Cahill, green-bodied Grasshopper and large Gray, Black, and Brown Wulffs, sizes 10-14. These same patterns work well for brook trout. One of the best landlocked salmon and brook trout rivers in Maine. Extremely remote; many sections reachable only by foot trail.

Moose Pond, Denmark. Bs. Best times, mid-May through June. Productive flies—Muddler, Woolly Worms, imitation mice, and terrestrial insects. Moose Pond holds current state record on smallmouth bass: 11 lbs. 7 oz. Fish coves and off points and sandbars.

*Pond-in-the-River and Rapid River, Twp. C. FFO. LL, BkT. Best times, mid-May through July; September. Productive flies—streamers: White and Yellow Marabous, Gray Ghost; dry: Henryville Special, Montana, Kennebago, and Coachman Wulffs, Hairwing Caddis, Gray Fox, Gray Caddis, Humpy, orange-,yellow-,and green-bodied Grasshoppers, Light Cahill, Hendrickson, Adams, Quill Gordon, sizes 10-16. The Rapid River is one of the best salmon and native brook trout rivers in Maine. It is extremely rapid and action depends on water flow. There is a good May fly and caddis fly hatch in June and early July. Accessible only by boat from South Arm.

*Richardson Ponds, East, Adamstown Twp. FFO. BkT. Best times, late May, June. Productive flies—dry: Mosquito, Gray Fox, Adams, Hendrickson, Black Gnat, Light Cahill, size 12-14. Accessible by foot trail or air only.

PENOBSCOT COUNTY

*Bowlin Pond, T.5,R.8. FFO. BkT. Best times, mid-May through late June; July in evenings; September. Productive flies—wet: Mickey Finn, Black Nose Dace, Light Edson Tiger, size 8; dry: Mosquito, Adams, orange-bodied Grasshopper, Light Cahill, March Brown, size 12.

*Ireland Pond, T.7,R.8.** NLFAB. BkT. Best times, mid-May through late June. September. Productive flies—dry: orange-bodied Grasshopper, Light Cahill, Dark Cahill, Mosquito, Black Gnat, size 12-14.

*Jones Pond, T.7,R.8.** NLFAB. BkT. Best times, mid-May through late June; July in evenings. Productive flies—dry: orange-bodied Grasshopper, Mosquito, March Brown, Adams, Black Gnat, size 12. Best reached by air from Patten.

*Messer Pond, Little, T.5,R.8.** NLFAB. BkT. Best times, mid-May through late June; July in evenings. Productive flies—dry: Mosquito, Adams, orange-bodied Grasshopper, size 12. Best reached by air from Patten.

*Mud Pond, T.2,R.8.** NLFAB. BkT. Best times, mid-May through late June; July in evenings; September. Productive flies—dry: Mosquito, Adams, March Brown, Quill Gordon, Light Cahill, orange-bodied Grasshopper, size 12-14. Best reached by air from Patten.

*Rocky Pond, T.3,R.8.** NLFAB. BkT. Best times, mid-May through late June; July in evenings; September. Productive flies—dry: Mosquito, Light Cahill, March Brown, orange-bodied Grasshopper, Light Hendrickson, size 12-14.

Sandy Stream, T.2,R.8. LL, BkT. Best times, mid-May through late June; September. Productive flies—wet: Gray Ghost, Black Ghost, Nine-Three, Mickey Finn, size 6-8; dry: Adams, Light Cahill, Mosquito, Grizzly Wulff, Gray Wulff, Light Hendrickson, size 10-14; nymphs: all May fly and caddis nymphs in natural colors, size 12-14. Offers good stream fishing for both salmon and trout.

Seboeis River, T.6,R.7. LL, BkT. Best times, mid-May through late July; September. Productive flies—wet: Mickey Finn, Gray Ghost, Black Ghost, Black Nose Dace, size 6-8; dry: Adams, orange-bodied Grasshopper, Light Cahill, Dark Cahill, Mosquito, March Brown, Gray Wulff, Gray Fox, size 10-14; nymphs in all natural colors are productive, size 12-14. The Seboeis offers good angling for both salmon and trout. Sections are heavily fished by bait fishermen and must be worked slowly and carefully for results.

*Trout Pond, T.2,R.7.** NLFAB. BkT. Best times, mid-May through late June; July in evenings. Productive flies—dry: orange-bodied Grasshopper, Mosquito, Light Cahill, Adams, March Brown, size 12-14.

PISCATAQUIS COUNTY

Allagash Pond, T.9,R.15. FFO. BkT. Best times, late May through early July in the evening. Productive flies—wet: Black Nose Dace, Light Edson Tiger, Dark Edson Tiger, size 8; dry: Dark Cahill, Dark Hendrickson, Mosquito, Black Gnat, Hare's Ear, March Brown, size 12-14. Do not mistake Allagash Pond for Allagash Lake. This pond is accessible by vehicle through the Caucomgomac gatehouse of the North Maine Woods.

*Blood (Duck) Pond, T.2,R.13.** FFO, no motorboats allowed. BkT. Best times, late May through June, mornings and evenings; through the rest of the season at dawn and dusk. Productive flies—wet: Muddler, Hornburg, Black Nose Dace, Light Edson Tiger, Dark Edson Tiger, size 8-10; dry: Adams, Light Cahill, Light Hendrickson, Mosquito, Black Gnat, size 12-14. Best reached by air from Greenville or Patten.

*Cranberry Pond, West Bowdoin College Grant.** FFO. BkT. Best times, mid-May through late June. Productive flies—wet: Muddler, Hornburg, Black Nose Dace, Black Gnat, Dark Edson Tiger, size 8-10; dry: Black Gnat, Mosquito, Dark Cahill,

Light Cahill, March Brown, Quill Gordon, size 10-14. Best reached by air from Greenville.

*Frost Pond, T.3,R.11. NLFAB, opens last Saturday in April. BkT. Best times, early May through mid-July evenings. Productive flies—wet: Muddler, Hornburg, Black Nose Dace, Dark Edson Tiger, size 8; dry: Black Gnat, Dark Hendrickson, Mosquito, March Brown, size 10-14. There is a set of private sporting camps on Frost Pond. Canoe launching is possible elsewhere, however.

*Frost Pond, Little, T.3,R.12. NLFAB, BkT. Best times, mid-May through the season, evenings. Productive flies—wet: same as for Big Frost; dry: same as for Big Frost, but add Quill Gordon. Fishing generally better than Big Frost. Accessible only by foot trail.

*Harrington Pond, T.3,R.11. FFO. BkT. Best times, mid-May through early July, mornings and evenings. Productive flies—wet: Muddler, Hornburg, Black Nose Dace, Dark Edson Tiger, size 8-10; dry: Adams, Black Gnat, Dark Hendrickson, Dark Cahill, Hare's Ear, size 12-14. Accessible by foot trail from the south end of Harrington Lake.

*Horseshoe Pond, West Bowdoin College Grant. FFO. BkT. Best times, early May through early July evenings. Productive flies—wet: Muddler, Black Nose Dace, Light Edson Tiger, Dark Edson Tiger, size 8-10; dry: Mosquito, Black Gnat, Dark Cahill, Dark Hendrickson, size 12-14. Best reached by air from Greenville.

Island Pond, T.9,R.10. LL, BkT. Best times, mid-May through late June, mornings and evenings. Productive flies—wet: Gray Ghost, Nine-Three, Black Nose Dace, Mickey Finn, Dark Edson Tiger; dry: Adams, Light Hendrickson, Light Cahill, Mosquito, Black Gnat, size 10-14. Can be reached by vehicle through the Six Mile Gatehouse of North Maine Woods. Also reached by air from Patten.

*Mountain Brook Pond, West Bowdoin College Grant. FFO. BkT. Best times, mid-May through early July, mornings and evenings. Productive flies—wet: Muddler, Hornburg, Black Nose Dace, Light Edson Tiger, size 8-10, dry: Black Gnat, Mosquito, Light Cahill, Light Hendrickson, March Brown, size 10-14. Best reached by air from Greenville.

*Nesowadnehunk Lake, T.4,R.10. FFO. BkT. Best times, late May through mid-June; September. Productive flies—wet: Muddler, Hornburg, Tri-Color, Black Nose Dace, Light Edson Tiger, Dark Edson Tiger; dry: Mosquito, Black Gnat, Adams, March Brown, Light Cahill, Light Hendrickson, size 10-14. This is one of the best brook trout waters in Maine. It is under heavy fishing pressure but some large trout are possible. Best fishing with wet flies starts around Memorial Day. Action with dry flies starts in early June. Fish calm shore during a wind when using dry flies.

*Nesowadnehunk Lake, Little, T.5,R11. FFO, No outboard motors allowed, daily limit two trout. BkT. Best times, late May through the season, particularly June, in early afternoons and evenings. Productive flies—dry: Mosquito, Adams, March Brown, Light Cahill, Light Hendrickson, Quill Gordon, Dark Cahill, Dark Hendrickson. This is one of the best brook trout waters within easy reach. Offers excellent fishing for large trout. Rated one of the best in the state. A half-mile mile hike is required.

*Trout Pond, Little Squaw Mt. Twp. FFO. BkT. Best times, mid-May through late June, mornings and evenings. Productive flies—dry: Mosquito, Black Gnat, March Brown, Dark Cahill, Dark Hendrickson, size 12-14. Can be reached by vehicle from Route 15.

*Wadleigh Pond, T.8,R.15. NLFAB. BkT. Best times, mid-May through early July, mornings and evenings. Productive flies—wet: Muddler, Black Nose Dace, Light Edson Tiger, size 8-10; dry: Mosquito, Light Cahill, Light Hendrickson, Black Gnat, March Brown. Can be reached by vehicle through the Caucomgomac Gatehouse of the North Maine Woods.

SOMERSET COUNTY

*Baker Pond, T.4,R.6. FFO. BkT. Best times, mid-May through late June; throughout season at dawn and dusk. Productive flies—dry: green-bodied Grasshopper, Mosquito, March Brown, Adams, Light Cahill, Black Gnat, size 12-14. Baker Pond is surrounded by private lands and can only be reached by plane from Jackman or Greenville. Provides excellent opportunity for large native trout.

*Berry Ponds Big and Little, Johnson Mtn. Twp. FFO. BkT. Best times, mid-May to late June. Productive flies—wet: Black Nose Dace, Light Edson Tiger, size 8-10; dry: Dark Cahill, Mosquito, Black Gnat, Adams, size 12-14.

*Bill Morris Pond, T.3,R.5. NLFAB. BkT. Best times, early or mid-May to early June. Productive flies—wet: March Brown, Blue Dun, Hare's Ear, Iron Blue Dun, size 10-12; dry: Iron Blue Dun, Ginger Quill, Light Cahill, Quill Gordon, March Brown, Mosquito, size 12-14.

*Cold Stream Pond, T.2,R.6. FFO. BkT. Best times, late May through July in evening. Productive flies—wet: Professor, Woolly Worm, Gray Hackle, Parmachene Belle, Coachman, size 12-14; dry: Adams, Light Cahill, Light Hendrickson, March Brown, Black Gnat, size 12-14.

*Dingley Ponds The Three, T.4,R.5. FFO. BkT. Best times, mid-May through late June. Productive flies—Adams, Light Cahill, Light Hendrickson, Mosquito. The Dingleys are accessible only by air from Jackman or Greenville. They are located only a few miles from the Canadian border and offer excellent fishing.

*Durgin Pond, Johnson Mtn. Twp. FFO. BkT. Best times, mid-May through June. Productive flies—Black Gnat, Mosquito, Adams, March Brown, Light Cahill, size 12-14.

*Ellis Pond, 10,000 Acre Tract. FFO. BkT. Best times, late May through mid July; August in evening; September. Productive flies—dry: Gray Hackle, olive-bodied Grasshopper, March Brown, Adams, Dark Cahill, Black Gnat, Dark Hendrickson, Mosquito, Gray Wulff, size 12-14. Ellis Pond has a good hatch of dark May flies in June, natural size 12. All dark mayfly imitations work well.

*Enchanted Pond, Little, Upper Enchanted Twp. FFO. BkT. Best times, mid-May through July in evening. Productive flies—dry: green-bodied Grasshopper, Black Gnat, Mosquito, size 10-14. Little Enchanted is accessible only by air from Jackman or Greenville. Has an excellent trout fishery.

*Fry Pan Pond, Squaretown Twp. FFO. BkT. Best times, mid-May through June. Productive flies—Black Gnat, Mosquito, March Brown, Adams, Light Cahill, size 12-14.

*Grace Pond, T.3,R.6. FFO. BkT. Best times, from ice-out through late June; July, August, and September at dawn and dusk. Productive flies—wet: Light Edson Tiger, Black Nose Dace; dry: March Brown, Dark Cahill, Dark Hendrickson, Adams, Gray

Wulff, size 12-14. Grace Pond offers fine spring and summer fishing. Access is restricted via a private set of sporting camps—fee required for launching.

Kennebec River, The Forks to Caratunk. LL, BkT. Best times, late July and August. Productive flies—wet: Nine-Three, Gray Ghost, size 8; dry: Royal Coachman, Blue Dun, Adams, Black Gnat, Mosquito, size 12-14. Because of the Kennebec's size and fluctuations, fishing can be slow. Some fine salmon and brook trout are available to the patient angler.

*Kennebec River (West and East Outlets from Moosehead Lake). East Outlet—artificial lures only. West Outlet—general law. LL, BkT. Best times, May through September. Productive flies—wet and streamers: Gray Ghost, Nine-Three, Supervisor, Pink Lady, Red Gray Ghost, size 6-8; dry: White Wulff, Coachman Wulff, Light Cahill, Blue Dun, size 10-14. These two stretches offer a combination of whitewater and deadwater areas; excellent fly fishing waters for both species. Action depends upon water level, however.

*Kilgore Pond, T.1,R.4. FFO. BkT. Best times, from ice-out (early May) through early June; September. Productive flies—dry: Gray Hackle, green-bodied Grasshopper, Black Gnat, Gray Wulff, Adams, size 12-14.

*Rock Pond, T.5,R.6. FFO. BkT. Best times, mid-May through early July in evening. Productive flies—dry: Green Drake, March Brown, Montana Wulff, Kennebago Wulff, Blue Wing Olive Dun, Green Humpy, Adams, Light Cahill, White Wulff, size 10-12. Rock Pond has a gigantic hatch of May flies each June. The naturals are size 10, and are creamy white in color. Other May flies and caddis emerge sporadically also.

*Split Rock Pond, Pierce Pond Twp. FFO. BkT. Best times, May through late June evenings. Productive flies—dry: Adams, Light Cahill, Black Gnat, Mosquito, size 12-14.

*Spring Lake, T.3,R.4. NLFAB. LL, Best times, from ice-out (mid-May) through late June. Productive flies—streamers: Gray Ghost, Black Ghost, Nine-Three, size 6-8; dry: Adams, March Brown, Dark Cahill, Red Quill, size 12-16. This is basically a lake for trolling streamer flies. Some salmon are taken on the surface, however, during a hatch.

WASHINGTON COUNTY

*Grand Lake Stream, Grand Lake Stream Plt. FFO. LL, BkT. Best times, mid-May; June; July in mornings and evenings; September. Productive flies—wet: Gray Ghost, Black Ghost, Nine-Three, Joe's Smelt, Ranger, Grand Laker, size 4-8; dry: Gold Ribbed Hare's Ear, Gray Caddis, Gray Fox, Muddler, size 10-12. Grand Lake Stream is rated one of the best salmon and brook trout rivers in the state, equally as productive as the Rapid, Kennebago, or West Branch. Nymphs work well here; all caddis and May fly patterns in natural shades; brown, olive, cream, black, and gray.

*Ledge Pond, Charlotte. NLFAB. BkT. Best times, early May through late June. Productive flies—dry: Black Ant, Light Hendrickson, Light Cahill, Adams, size 12.

*Monroe Lake, T.43,MD. NLFAB. BkT. Best times, early May through June; September. Productive flies—dry: Black Gnat, Black Ant, Dark Hendrickson, Gray Wulff, size 10-14.

*Ox-Brook Lake, Upper and Lower, Talmadge. NLFAB. BkT. Best times, early May through June; July in evenings; September. Productive flies—dry: Dark Cahill, Black Ant, Dark Hendrickson, Black Gnat, size 12-16.

YORK COUNTY

*Deer Pond, Hollis. Daily limit five trout, opens last Saturday in April. BrT. Best times, early May or right after ice-out; during June at dusk. Productive flies—In May, small wet flies close to the bottom. Later, dry flies resembling hatch will produce. Recommend Light Cahill, Gray Fox, and Hendrickson, size 14. There are some good brown trout in Deer Pond, but productivity is slow.

*Ossipee Lake, Little, Waterboro. Two fish daily limit in aggregate of salmon and togue, no size or bag limit on bass. LL, Bs. Best times, for salmon, early May through mid-June; for bass, mid-May through August. Productive flies—double hooked streamer patterns. Red and White Bucktail, Muddler, and Woolly Worm for bass.

Ossipee River, Big, Kezar Falls to Saco River BrT. Best times, late May and June. Productive flies—Henryville Special, Gray Caddis, Humpy Hairwing Caddis, Light Cahill, size 10. Work above and below the rapid areas, best reached with a canoe. Large eddy areas are recommended.

Saco River, Hiram to Limington. BrT. Best times, late May and June. Productive flies—Henryville Special, Gray Caddis, Humpy, Hairwing Caddis, size 12-14. Large browns are possible from the Saco, but finding action is difficult due to the river's size and diverse habitat. Watch rapid and close deadwater areas.

*Sand Pond, Limington. NLFAB, daily limit five fish, opens last Saturday in April. BkT. Best times, June and September. Productive flies—brownish or creamish nymphs; wet: Hendrickson and Light Cahill.

*Spicer Pond, Shapleigh. Daily limit, three trout. BkT. Best times, from mid-June to end of season. Productive flies—light yellow and green nymphs; yellow- and green-bodied Grasshoppers. Cannot be reached by automobile.

*Wadley Pond, Lyman. No size or bag limit on bass. Bs. Best time, early May through mid-June. Productive flies—Mickey Finn, Red and White Bucktail, Muddler. Wadley's is loaded with small bass; large specimens taken on occasion.

MISCELLANEOUS WATERS

Cobbosseecontee Lake (Kennebec County), E. Winthrop. Bs. Best times, early May through June. Productive flies—wet: Mickey Finn, Red and White Bucktail; bright colored poppers, size 6-8. Rated one of the best black bass waters in the Northeast.

*Ducktrap River (Waldo County), Lincolnville. FFO. BkT. Best times, early May through late June; September. Productive flies—wet: Black Nose Dace, Light Edson Tiger, Mickey Finn size 6-10; dry: Adams, Light Cahill, March Brown, size 12.

*Hastings Pond (Lincoln County), Bristol. FFO. BkT. Best times, late April through June. Productive flies—dry: Adams, Light Cahill, Black Gnat, Mosquito, March Brown, size 12-14.

Messalonskee Lake (Kennebec County), Winthrop. Bs. Best times, early May through June. Productive flies—wet: Mickey Finn, Red and White Bucktail, size 6-8; Imitation terrestrial insect; ants, grasshoppers, moths.

THE WATERS WITHIN BAXTER

The following is a list of trout ponds and streams within Baxter State Park in Piscataquis County. While many are not restricted to fly fishing only (many are), utilization of flies in most cases will produce better results. Fly fishing only for trout in the park is highly recommended not only for the results, but also for helping protect a fragile resource in a unique area.

You will note that many of the ponds are accessible only by foot trail. It should be remembered that there are no canoes on most parks ponds; those where canoes and lodging are available have been so indicated. However, because many of these waters are shallow and drop at a slow rate, good fishing is usually possible with just a pair of waders.

Many of the waters within Baxter State Park are open to general law fishing. This is done primarily to offer the entire angling fraternity a chance to fish in a truly unique and wilderness-type setting. Some waters, however, are restricted to fly fishing only—these are for the most part located in the southwestern corner of the park and south of Nesowadnehunk Lake.

Those waters not restricted should not be neglected by the fly fisherman, however. These ponds and streams have strong, healthy May fly hatches and offer excellent and productive angling throughout much of the season. Overall, Baxter State Park is a fly fisherman's haven, though laws and regulations indicate otherwise.

It should be remembered while traveling within Baxter that wildlife can be found everywhere. Moose are often encountered walking the gravel roads, and they often share the ponds and streams with fishermen. Bear, while not as commonly seen, are frequent sights and should be given a wide berth, as should all wildlife.

It is highly recommended that parties anticipating a camping/fishing trip to Baxter State Park plan their excursion well in advance of departure date, even if they are familiar with the park and its rules and regulations. Further information may be obtained by writing to the park headquarters in Millinocket. For the address and telephone number check in this book under "SOURCES OF INFORMATION".

*Daicey Pond. FFO. BkT. Best times, mid-May through late June; September. Productive flies—wet: Mickey Finn, Black Nose Dace, size 8-10; dry: Adams, Light Cahill, Light Hendrickson, Mosquito, Gray Wulff, orange-bodied Grasshopper, size 10-12. This is a good wet fly pond early in the spring and throughout the season when trout are not active on the surface. Camps rented by the Baxter State Park Authority are available, as are canoes. Reservations recommended.

*Deep Pond. NLFAB. BkT. Best times, mid-May through June to mid-July; September. Productive flies—dry: Light Cahill, Light Hendrickson, Adams, Mosquito, yellow-bodied Grasshopper, size 12. Deep Pond is located a half-mile from Russell Pond. The water is dark; light flies or flies with bright bodies work the best. Canoes may be rented from the ranger at Russell.

*Draper Pond. NLFAB. BkT. Best times, late May through June; early July; September. Productive flies—Adams, Light Cahill, Light Hendrickson, orange-bodied Grasshopper, March Brown, size 12. No marked trail, but can be reached from Russell Pond; ask ranger for directions. Has some excellent trout, however. No canoes— difficult to fish.

*Foss & Knowlton Pond. FFO. BkT. Best times, mid-May through mid-June; in July during evenings, September. Productive flies—dry: Adams, Mosquito, Light Cahill, Light Hendrickson, March Brown, orange-bodied Grasshopper, size 12. Foss & Knowlton Pond is located on the southern border of the park. Although a trail from Katahdin Stream Campground offers access, it can now be reached via a fire road near the Abol Store bridge on the West Branch of the Penobscot River.

*Fowler Pond, Little. NLFAB. BkT. Best times, late May through June. Productive flies—dry: Mosquito, Adams, Light Cahill, Light Hendrickson, orange bodied Grasshopper, March Brown, size 12-14. Best reached from Trout Brook area. Has some large trout, but fishing may be slow at times. Check with ranger at Trout Brook Campground for canoe information.

*Nesowadnehunk Stream. FFO. BkT. Best times, late May through July; September. Productive flies—nymphs: all May fly nymphs in brown, olive, cream, tan, and black; wet: Mickey Finn, Black Nose Dace, Dark Hendrickson, Dark Cahill, size 8-10; dry: Adams, Light Cahill, Light Hendrickson, Mosquito, March Brown, orange-bodied Grasshopper, Grizzly Wulff, Gray Wulff, size 10-12. Nesowadnehunk Stream offers the best stream fishing in the park. It offers a range of waters from deep pools to fast water to fantastic eddy areas. This is a fine stream for the nymph fisherman early in the spring, and wet flies are producers in mid-May. Use large dry flies in the riffle areas and over the deep pools and pockets in June and July. Action depends upon water flow throughout the season.

*Pogy Pond. NLFAB. BkT. Best times, late May through early June. Productive flies—wet: Mickey Finn, Gray Ghost, Black Ghost, Nine-Three, size 6-8. This pond is best early in the spring for trolling streamers; must paddle canoes since no motors are allowed. Use sinking line and fish very deep. Pogy Pond has some very fine trout. Canoes may be rented from rangers as Russell Pond or at South Branch Pond.

*Russell Pond. NLFAB. BkT. Best times, late May through July, (mid-July is best); September. Productive flies—dry: Green Drake, green-bodied Grasshopper, green-bodied Humpy, Mosquito, Royal Coachman, Wulff, Dark Hendrickson, size 10-12. Russell Pond is one of the best dry fly trout ponds within Baxter. Action starts with floating offerings right after ice-out and lasts until the end of July; it picks up again in September. Russell experiences a gigantic Green Drake hatch in late June and July and the imitation with the same name is effective. But because of the activity of rising trout at that time, any large May fly imitation will produce. Canoes and lean-tos available. A seven-mile hike is required from Roaring Brook.

*Six Ponds. NLFAB. BkT. Best times, mid-May through early July; September. Productive flies—dry: Adams, Light Cahill, Light Hendrickson, Mosquito, orange- and green-bodied Grasshoppers, size 12. Located 1.5 miles from Russell Pond. Has a good May fly hatch during dates given. Canoes may be rented from the ranger at Russell Pond.

*Trout Brook. NLFAB. BkT. Best times, mid-May through early July; September. Productive flies—nymphs: all May fly nymphs in brown, olive, cream, tan, and black; wet: Mickey Finn, Black Nose Dace, size 8-10; dry: Gray Wulff, Grizzly Wulff, Mosquito, Adams, Light Cahill, Light Hendrickson, size 10-12. Found along the northern stretch of the perimeter road. A good mixture of water best suited for wet flies and dry flies. Larger dries are best in riffle areas and deep pools on a long drift.

*Twin Pond. NLFAB. BkT. Best times, late May through early July; September. Productive flies—orange-bodied Grasshopper, Dark Hendrickson, Dark Cahill, Mosquito, March Brown, size 12. Located on the eastern border of the park. May be reached by a cut-off trail from either Russell Pond or Roaring Brook. Also reached by a road from Stacyville; hard to find. Has some fine trout, but may not be worth the effort considering other ponds in the area.

*Wassataquoik Pond, Little. NLFAB. BkT. Best times, mid-May through early July; September. Productive flies—Light Cahill, Dark Cahill, Light Hendrickson, Adams, orange-bodied Grasshopper, Mosquito, size 12. Reached from Russell Pond. Has some fine trout. Lean-to available; may be rented from ranger at Russell Pond. Ask ranger for canoe information.

QUIMBY POND

Rangeley Twp.,
Franklin County
Area: 165 acres
Maximum depth: 12 feet
Game species: brook
trout, brown trout

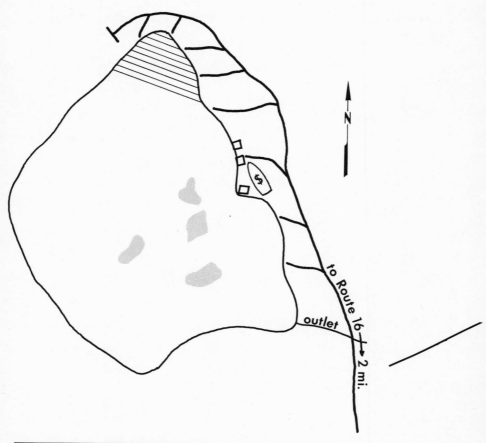

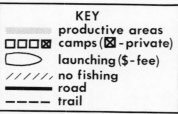

KEY
productive areas
☐☐☐☒ camps (☒ - private)
launching ($ - fee)
/ / / / / no fishing
road
trail

ROUND MOUNTAIN POND

Alder Stream Twp.,
Franklin County
Area: 75 acres
Maximum depth: 35 feet
Game species: brook trout

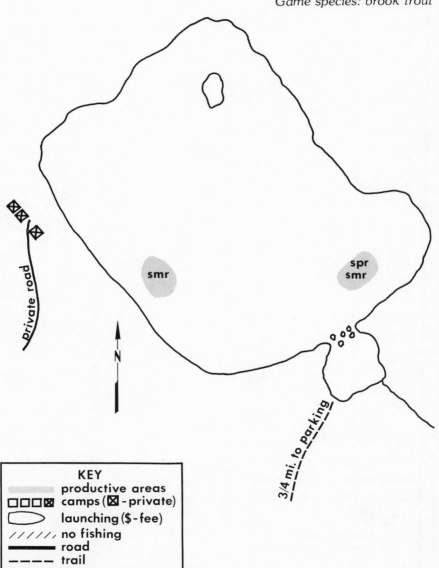

private road

smr

spr
smr

N

3/4 mi. to parking

KEY

▦	productive areas
☐☐☐☒	camps (☒ - private)
⬭	launching ($ - fee)
//////	no fishing
▬▬	road
- - - -	trail

NESOWADNEHUNK LAKE

T4, R10 & R11; T5, R10 & R11, Piscataquis County
Area: 1394 acres
Maximum depth: 46 feet
Game species: brook trout

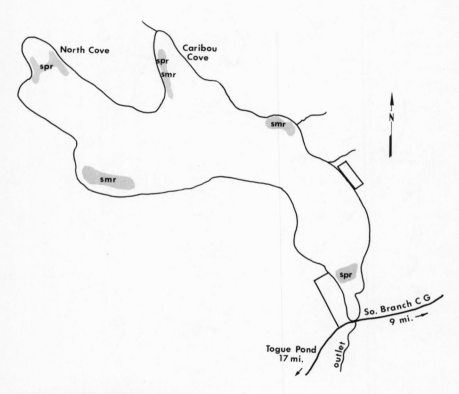

North Cove

Caribou Cove

spr

spr

smr

smr

smr

spr

N

So. Branch C G
9 mi.

Togue Pond
17 mi.

outlet

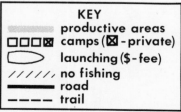

KEY
productive areas
□□□☒ camps (☒ - private)
launching ($ - fee)
////// no fishing
road
---- trail

LITTLE NESOWAD-
NEHUNK LAKE

T5, R11, Piscataquis
County
Area: 102 acres
Maximum depth: 15 feet
Game species: brook trout

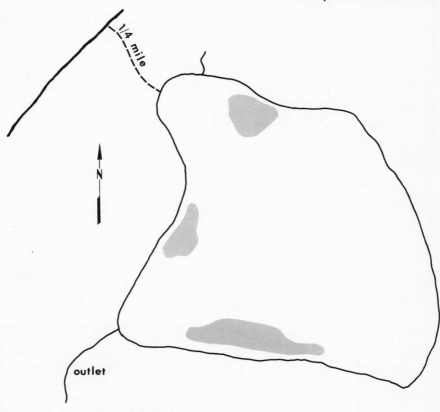

outlet

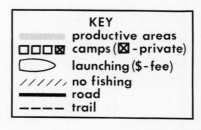

KEY
productive areas
☐☐☐☒ camps (☒ - private)
⬭ launching ($ - fee)
/////// no fishing
—————— road
— — — — trail

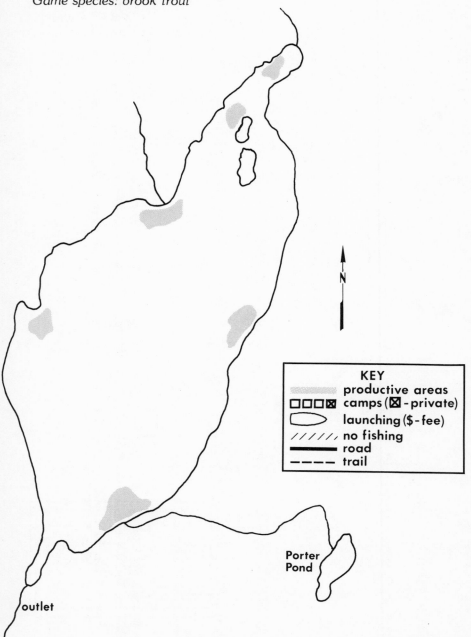

BAKER POND

T5, R6, Somerset County
Area: 240 acres
Maximum depth: 33 feet
Game species: brook trout

N

KEY
productive areas
camps (⊠ - private)
launching ($ - fee)
////// no fishing
road
----- trail

Porter
Pond

outlet

BILL MORRIS POND

T3, R5, Somerset County
Area: 23 acres
Maximum depth: 23 feet
Game species: brook trout

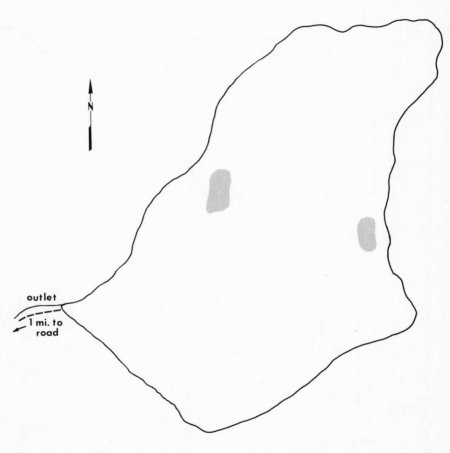

outlet

1 mi. to
road

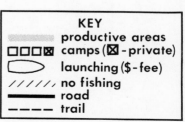

KEY
productive areas
□□□⊠ camps (⊠ - private)
launching ($ - fee)
///// no fishing
road
----- trail

COLDSTREAM POND

T2, R6 & R7; T3, R7,
*   Somerset County*
Area: 205 acres
Maximum depth: 62 feet
Game species: brook trout

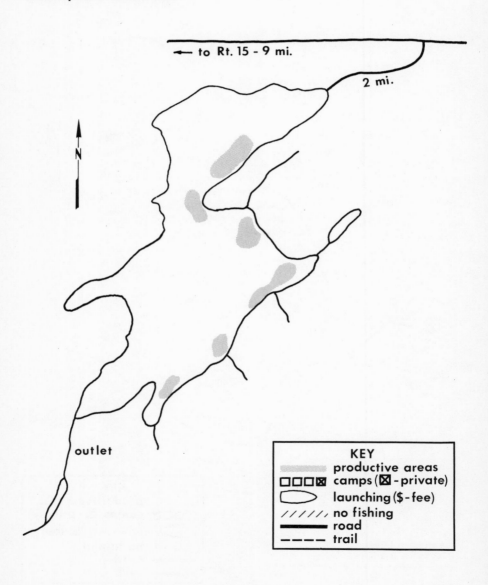

← to Rt. 15 - 9 mi.

2 mi.

N

outlet

KEY
productive areas
camps (⊠ - private)
launching ($ - fee)
/////// no fishing
road
---- trail

ELLIS POND

T1, R6, Somerset County
Area: 85 acres
Maximum depth: 38 feet
Game species: brook trout

Duck Cove

N

fl

fl

to Rt. 201
← 7 mi.

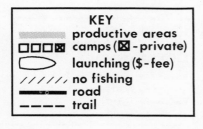

KEY
productive areas
camps (⊠ - private)
launching ($ - fee)
////// no fishing
road
----- trail

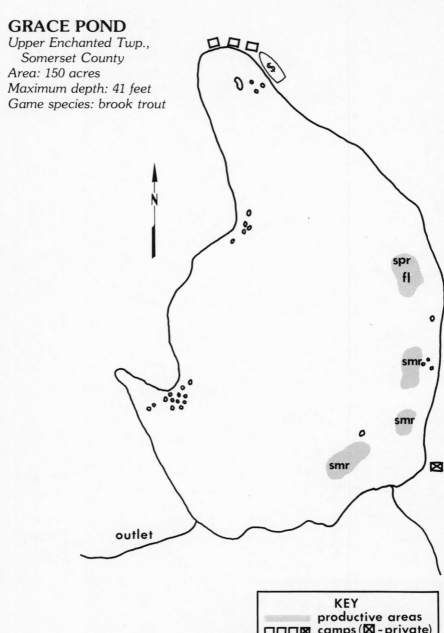

GRACE POND

Upper Enchanted Twp.,
  Somerset County
Area: 150 acres
Maximum depth: 41 feet
Game species: brook trout

N

spr
fl

smr

smr

smr

outlet

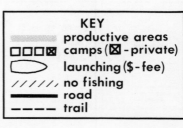

KEY

productive areas
camps (⊠ - private)
launching ($ - fee)
no fishing
road
trail

RUSSELL POND

T4, R9, Piscataquis County
(Baxter State Park)
Area: 20 acres
Maximum depth: 6 feet
Game species: brook trout

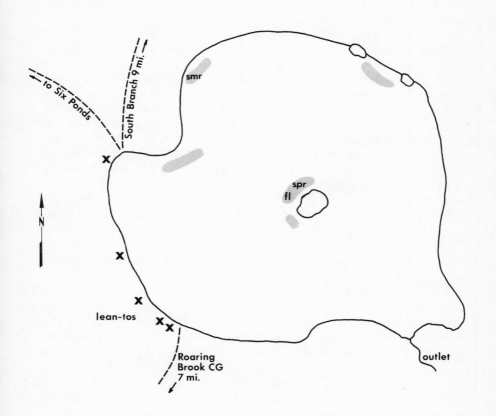

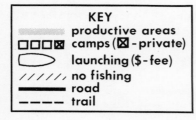

KEY
productive areas
camps (⊠ - private)
launching ($ - fee)
no fishing
road
trail

A WORD ON SALTWATER BROWNS

In May of 1976, the Sebago Lake regional office of the Maine Department of Inland Fisheries and Wildlife released 8,500 six-inch brown trout fingerlings into the Ogunquit and Royal Rivers. The Ogunquit, located in York County, got 1,000 while the Royal in Cumberland County received 7,500 fish. This was done in hopes of establishing a sea run brown trout fishery such as those which had proven successful in no less than seven Massachusetts rivers in the mid-1960s and early 1970s.

Subsequent releases took place in the springs of 1977, 1978, and 1979, with continued stocking planned for the future. While no in-depth biological studies have been conducted, it appears that, after four years of minimum stocking effort, Maine is well on the way to possessing a highly impressive and healthy sea run brown trout fishery.

The salt water brown is unlike its fresh water brother is several respects. From an angling viewpoint, salt browns seem to be less selective towards artificial offerings, and they seem to be on a constant feeding binge-these factors are most important. There are a number of biological differences as well, however, the most important being a rapid and phenomenal growth rate.

The six-inch fingerlings released into the Ogunquit River in May of 1976, for example, weighed only a couple of ounces apiece. By mid-October of the same year, however, anglers were catching specimens measuring 14 to 15 inches, some weighing as much as one and one-half pounds. This represents roughly 1.4 inches of growth per month throughout the summer, compared to the average half-inch of growth per month of fresh water browns. Thus far, the largest sea run brown taken on rod and reel weighed just over seven pounds. It was stocked in the Royal River in 1977 and was caught in the fall of 1978!

When biologists first released brown trout into Maine tidal waters, it was believed that they would exhibit typical anadromous characteristics, spending their early days within the estuary, then running out to sea and returning as mature adults. This has not proven to be the case, at least so far.

As an angling foe, the salt water brown is a challenge and a battling dynamo. Though not as selective or cautious as the fresh water brown, the sea runner must be presented with sinking artificials resembling his natural forage before action will be received. Once hooked, however, his belligerence commands respect. Several casts are often required, however, before the take.

The estuarial brown is selective in the *size* of the food he consumes, and therefore in the size of the imitation he will accept. Natural bait two inches or less in length is preferred, so flies of this size are best; this means, roughly, hook sizes 4 through 10, not including the overlap of the wing. Patterns with feathers or bucktail trimmed even with the end of the hook work better than those with wings extending past the "shape", or bend, in the hook.

Several productive patterns have been discovered by local fishermen. The Muddler Minnow is one of the best, but the Grass-Shrimp pattern lying on the bottom produces fine results as well. Both should be utilized in size 6 or 8, although the Shrimp sometimes produces well in size 10, also.

Some contemporary designs such as the Gray Ghost and Black Ghost will produce results, as will bucktail combinations with white and brown or white and black carrying tinsel bodies. I usually tie in a red tail or red wool tag.

Again, these patterns are fished wet, or below the surface. A floating line with a sinking tip, equipped with at least a four-pound test leader, is recommended; the leader does not have to be tapered, although technical enthusiasts follow the gospel and utilize tapered tippets. The flies do not have to be worked fast, but a "jerking" method often induces acceptance. When the fly is taken, simply raise the tip of the rod, keeping the line taut.

If the brown is of any size and weight, he'll undoubtedly want to run and is apt to break water in typical "salmonid" style. Keep the line taut with some strain behind it at all times, but do not overpower the fish. As with landlocked or Atlantic salmon, a powerful jerk of the head can break the leader.

Because the sea run brown is found in estuarial habitat, the hours in which anglers may seek him are limited. At high tide, both the Ogunquit and lower Royal rivers are fairly wide and deep, allowing plenty of room for them to roam. Therefore, dead low tide offers the best chances once they have been forced into the pools.

Generally, the hours before, during, and immediately after low tide are best. Waders are helpful in reaching some of the best vantage points, particularly when fighting the wind.

As mentioned earlier, it has been discovered that salt water browns stay within the estuary throughout the year in Maine. Peak activity, however, is in mid-October, once cool water is flowing downriver; late summer or early fall rains can keep the fish in deep water close to the ocean. But as a rule, fish are being seen or taken regularly by the 15th of October. Activity will continue through November and into December, at which time feeding appears to slow somewhat and cold weather keeps fishermen away from the water.

The salt water brown is truly a magnificent sportfish, and Maine is indeed fortunate to have two rivers producing such excellent specimens. If the current trend continues, we will be seeing two- and three-pound examples regularly, and the dedicated fly fisherman will have at his fingertips a trophy fishery once inland waters have closed for the season.

Chapter 7
FLYING AND HIKING INTO REMOTE PONDS

Flying In

Fifty years ago, the northern and western woodlands of Maine were a true wilderness compared to what they are today. In this age the term "wilderness" is over-emphasized. In truth, much of the timber grown in this region has been cut at least once—in many areas, twice. Though still beautiful and vastly unspoiled, Maine technically houses a massive "semi-wilderness" which is changing, or at least being threatened by change, every day. As a fly fisherman and person who enjoys the outdoors a very great deal, this threat worries me.

In the "good ole days", it was possible to pack the automobile with camping and fishing gear and head off into the northern and western Maine wilderness with the assumption that productive fishing would be found. Old-timers have often testified about the massive brook trout taken from ponds which were then accessible only by foot trail, canoe, or careful navigation over abandoned tote roads.

"As a youngster," I have been told more than once, "it may be difficult to believe it was once like that, but it's true. It ain't today, though. Hell, today you can reach the Allagash in air-conditioned Cadillacs! They got roads leading everywhere in that country. And the fishin's showin' it, too."

With so much territory being opened to the recreationist, many of the remote trout ponds are becoming crowded and over-fished. The fisherman seeking a true wilderness experience, away from the multitudes of anglers and mobile campers who congregate where "the fishin's good", are turning more and more to float planes which can quickly get them to a secluded haven.

Since the late 1950s, the bush pilot business has become a thriving and highly competitive industry in northern and western Maine. In towns such as Jackman, Greenville, and Millinocket, there is at least one seasonal establishment catering to the sportsman, and most often there are two or three—or more.

Smaller towns located on lakes scattered throughout this angling region support flying services as well. And, as the need for plane access grows, the industry is slowly becoming synonymous with Maine sporting life. There is little doubt that flying into remote areas for a wilderness experience is becoming more popular, for such an excursion is truly one of the most unique and thrilling adventures the sportsman can undertake.

While planning a fly-in fishing trip is not an overly difficult task, one should use common sense while arranging his excursion. It should always be kept in mind that once the plane lifts off, it is leaving you in a wild and remote world. There are no grocery stores, hospitals, restaurants, or help for miles around. A memorable trip—and even your life—depends a great deal on how well you're prepared and on the equipment you carry. Plan ahead, and be prepared for the unexpected.

Ideally, a remote fishing trip should be planned during the *winter* months, long before the open water season arrives. As early as February or March, letters should be sent out to flying services in the town closest to the area you want to fish. Indicate your intentions, ask for prices, weight quotas, and suggestions. Many of these pilots make their living from flying fishermen and sportsmen into remote areas. They are experienced, they expect questions, and they will help plan your trip so it will be a memorable experience.

One of the most frequently asked questions concerning flying into remote trout ponds is: "When are the best times to go?" The best productivity will unquestionably be found from June through the middle or latter part of July, after which time water temperatures force larger trout to greater depths and action can be slow.

September is often a productive month, particularly from about the 10th to the close of the season. On many of the northern and high altitude ponds in the western mountain area, the fall turnover comes early, drawing the larger trout back to the surface. Angling is excellent at this time, often better than in the spring.

It should be noted, however, that while the best fishing will usually be found during the dates just indicated, the majority of waters accessible only by air are much the way they were a century ago. They are underfished, maintain the best brook trout fishery remaining in the United States, and provide unparalleled angling.

Because of these facts, it is seldom that the visiting fly fisherman does not find action. During the warmer months of late July and August, I have had excellent luck during the early morning and late afternoon hours, particularly when a hatch is appearing. When the water is bare of emerging naturals, terrestrial and floating downwing imitations may save the day. But if an excursion is impossible for you during the "hot" periods, do not let this deter you from going. Chances are you will find excellent angling, and the chance to experience a remote fishing and camping trip should not be missed.

As mentioned earlier, it should always be remembered to plan a remote fishing trip well. Lists of food supplies, fishing tackle, and camping equipment should be made, checked, and rechecked. While lists of duffle will vary from group to group, certain things should be considered basic necessities. Here is a list of equipment nearly always carried by *parties* flying into remote ponds:

Tent (unless wilderness shelter is supplied by flying service)
Sleeping bags, plus extra blankets for cool-weather trips
Cooking and eating utensils
First aid kit
Insect repellent
Small cook stove
Lantern or battery-powered light (extra mantles, fuel, and/or batteries)
Matches (preferably waterproofed and windproof)
Compass and area maps
Food supplies
Canoe, paddles, and life jackets
Axe or hatchet

The following list is optional, containing items which can make a remote trip more enjoyable if room and weight allowance permits:

Air mattress or foam pad
Flashlight
Camera and film
Air mattress pump
Reflector oven

A list of personal items can be as long as an individual deems "necessary" But space and weight are factors when flying into remote areas, and only essentials should be carried. Even when restricted to *minimum* duffle and/or weight, however, those items followed by an asterisk (*) are still going with me. The list which follows is one which I follow when space and weight allows:

Underwear*
Socks* (at least one pair per day)
Pants* (at least three pair for the average week-long trip)
Shirts* (short sleeved shirts are fine, but do not offer much protection from insects and cold weather. Flannel or wool shirts are best)
Light jacket, sweater, or sweat shirts*
Rain gear*
Toilet kit* (toothbrush, toothpaste, soap, comb, shaving equipment, etc.)
Toilet tissue*
Towels and wash cloths*
Boots*
Compass*
Emergency match supply*
Insect repellent*
Jackknife*
Fishing equipment*
Shorts
Bathing suit
Sun glasses
Handkerchiefs
Pipe, tobacco, cigarettes
Light pair of gloves (for early- or late-season trips)
Flashlight
Camp moccasins

One of the most unique feelings a fisherman can experience comes after the plane has lifted off, leaving you on the shore of a remote pond miles from civilization. For the length of your stay, the food and equipment you carry must sustain you, so careful planning and rechecking before departure is imperative.

Menus for each meal should be scheduled ahead to make sure that sufficient food supplies are taken. First aid kits should be stocked, and compasses checked for accuracy. Sleeping bags and blankets and clothes are best carried in watertight plastic bags (plastic trash bags work well). And all equipment should be labeled or marked for easy and quick identification.

When planning meals, allow more than is necessary—"it is better to have it and not need it than to need it and not have it."

Always check your fishing gear carefully before leaving civilization. It's hell to be 80 miles from the nearest fly shop and discover that you're out of floating imitations—so carry a good supply of favorite patterns and types of terminal gear. Carry also a good supply of leaders, fly dressing, and line dressing. Fly lines, reels, and rods should be in good condition and are best carried in unbreakable containers.

Below is a list of what I consider essential fishing equipment:

Rod(s)
Reels(s) (at least one floating and one sinking line should be carried)
Fishing vest
Landing net
Assortment of wet and floating flies
Dry fly dressing
Line dressing
Leaders of preferred lengths and pound-tests
Fingernail clippers
Creel

On the shores of many northern ponds, camping and fire permits are required. Fire permits may be obtained free of charge at Maine Forest Service stations, found in most of the popular flying towns. Ponds located within the North Maine Woods may have *designated* campsites where no fire permits are needed, but a small daily or weekly fee is charged.

In your letter to the flying service, inquire about these permits. Once the trip has been confirmed, the service will usually secure the necessary permits and have them waiting when you arrive. Addresses of local Maine Forest Service stations and the North Maine Woods are listed under "SOURCES OF INFORMATION" in case you wish to obtain the permits in advance.

At the present time, there are numerous commercial flying services scattered throughout northern and western Maine. In order to assist you in planning your trip, I have included a list of the better establishments located in different areas of the state. It is recommended that one of these services be contacted regarding prices, weight limits, and other information not covered in this chapter.

JACKMAN AREA

Moose River Flying Service
Jackman, ME 04945
Telephone 207-668-2781

MOOSEHEAD LAKE AREA

Folsom's Air Service
Greenville, ME 04441
Telephone 207-695-2821

Jack's Air Service
Greenville, ME 04441
Telephone 207-695-3020

Moosehead Flying Service
Greenville Junction, ME 04442
Telephone 207-695-3345

MILLINOCKET AREA

Millinocket Flying Service
Ambajejus Lake
Millinocket, ME 04462
Telephone 207-723-8378

PATTEN AREA

Scotty's Flying Service
Shin Pond   Box 256-S
Patten, ME 04765
Telephone 207-528-2626

Porter's Flying Service
Shin Pond
Patten, ME 04765
Telephone 207-528-2528

PORTAGE LAKE AREA

Portage Lake Flying Service
Portage Lake, ME 04768
Telephone 207-435-6747

RANGELEY AREA

Steve's Air Service
Rangeley, ME 04970
Telephone 207-864-3347

GENERAL NORTHERN POINTS

Twitchell's Airport
Turner, ME 04282
Telephone 207-225-3490

Hiking In

For years, the mountain ranges which dot the western and north central forest lands of Maine have been recognized as some of the most popular hiking areas in the Northeast. Unlike the White Mountains of New Hampshire, much of this area is under-utilized by the hiking fraternity, the bulk of the attention going to certain stretches of the Appalachian Trail and trail system around Mt. Katahdin in Baxter State Park.

The fly fisherman who prefers to don a backpack and get into some of the mountain areas where aircraft and roads do not go is indeed lucky in Maine. For at his disposal are some truly magnificent trout waters which receive no angling pressure other than from those willing to carry their gear over miles of mountain trails and rough terrain. Those willing to accept such conditions are relatively few in the fishing spectrum. Thus, enthusiasts interested in both hiking and fly fishing often have these productive mountain waters to themselves.

Hiking into a remote mountain pond is, without question, one of the most rewarding ventures the fly fisherman and/or outdoor lover can undertake. The majority of these waters are situated in magnificently remote country which, because of its rough mountainous character, has not yet been scarred by the lumberman's axe. Moose, beaver, otter, deer, and a variety of birds are plentiful and usually unnaturally friendly towards man. The scenic surroundings—mountains, forests, and panoramic vistas—are unparalleled in beauty, and, with little effort, the outdoor recreationalist can really enjoy himself in this unique and solitary environment.

As for the fly fisherman, there is much for him to enjoy as well. The ponds, lakes, and major streams are crystal clear and are homes for healthy native brook trout fisheries. Many of the high-altitude waters are cold and deep; large trout are uncommon. But insect life is rich, and angling for native fish measuring between 10 and 12 inches is not unheard of—in many areas, it is fairly common.

The opportunity to have a whole pond to oneself often makes the efforts of hiking over a mountain ridge worthwhile. The solitude and serenity are amazingly relaxing and peaceful—the possible productive fishing and abundant wildlife are extra attractions thrown in!

Many of the best fishing opportunities for the hiker in Maine are found along the Appalachian Trail and within Baxter State Park. While it would seem that these two areas would be over-populated with hikers and fishermen, this is not necessarily true.

Baxter State Park, for example, is known as a hiker's paradise, but much of the pressure is on and around Mt. Katahdin. Inland areas around Russell Pond and Poggy Pond attract largely fishing enthusiasts. The Appalachian Trail, although heavily used in sections, is, for the most part, under-used in Maine. And several other areas are in the same situation. We will discover some of these hiking/fishing areas later on in this chapter.

But first, it is important that we know what to carry and who to contact for further information and necessary permits. While planning a hiking/fishing trip in Maine, it should be remembered that most waters are located far into rugged mountain country. All the food, clothing, and supplies needed during the journey must be carried on your back. You should carry nothing that is not required, keeping the pack as light as possible. A list of supplies and food should be made, making sure that all items are necessary—leave the rest behind!

Following is a list of equipment which I consider necessary:

Small nylon tent
Portable cook stove and fuel
Cooking and eating utensils
Pocket compass
Waterproof match supply
Canteen or water jug(s)
Clothing
Food
Guide book or trail map
Sleeping bag
Hatchet
Rubber raft and paddles
Rain gear
Fishing equipment (same as listed under "Flying In" section. Be sure to carry enough of everything, including flies of all patterns, fly dressing, leaders, etc.)
Flashlight
Insect repellent
First aid kit
Toilet kit (same as listed under "Flying In" section.)

Notice in the above list the mention of a rubber raft and paddles. Unlike a fly-in trip to a remote pond, canoes cannot be carried while hiking into a mountain hideaway, and, without some kind of boat, fishing would be restricted to casting from shore—not the most productive method.

A rubber or vinyl boat, therefore, is the most logical craft. The modern hiker/fly fisherman is fortunate, for at his fingertips are completely suitable rafts at economical prices, weighing from 12 pounds for a two-man unit to 15 pounds for a three-man craft. Smaller units with one-man capacity weigh as little as seven pounds. All models can be rolled tightly and carried in a regular backpack with other equipment, and are necessary if productive fishing is to be found, at least on the majority of the following waters.

The following list of ponds has been included in this chapter with the hopes of assisting the fly fishing enthusiast in choosing a relatively easily accessible, but still secluded, trout pond. While there are many other areas available, the following have been selected for their remote characteristics, easy access, and fine trout populations. It is not my intent to supply a complete hiking guide, but rather to encourage this type of recreation to that minority of fly fishermen who find the combination of these two great activities rewarding.

For detailed trail maps, distance and hiking time information, and exact locations of shelters and water supplied, it is recommended that interested persons purchase the A.M.C. MAINE MOUNTAIN GUIDE, which covers in detail all hiking trails in Maine, including the Appalachian Trail and trail systems in all state parks, including Baxter State Park. This book can be purchased from the Appalachian Mountain Club, 5 Joy Street, Boston, MA 02108. For additional information on hiking and fishing within Baxter State Park, write to the Baxter State Park Authority, Milinocket, Maine 04462, or telephone (207) 723-9616.

APPALACHIAN TRAIL

FROM: Rt. 26 at Grafton Notch; **TO:** Speck Pond; **DISTANCE in miles (one way):** 3; **HIKING TIME in hours (one way):** 3; **NOTES:** Lean-to available at pond which contains native brook trout. Ascent is extremely steep for first two miles; said to be most vertical hiking trail in Northeast. Pond is 3,500 feet above sea level; highest known pond in Maine containing trout!

FROM: Rt. 4 in Sandy River Township, Franklin County; **TO:** Eddy Pond; **DISTANCE in miles (one way):** 2; **HIKING TIME in hours (one way):** 1.5-2; **NOTES:** Easy hike with moderate climbs. Lean-to available 2 miles south of pond on A.T. Ethal Pond is found south of Eddy pond and allows good fishing.

FROM: Rt. 16/27 in Crockertown Township, Franklin County: **TO:** Stratton Brook Pond; **DISTANCE in miles (one way):** 3.5; **HIKING TIME in hours (one way):** 2-2.5; **NOTES:** Restricted to FFO. This is one of the best brook trout ponds along the A.T. in western Maine. No LEAN-TOS AVAILABLE. Easy hike with only moderate and gradual ascents.

WITHIN BAXTER STATE PARK

FROM: Trout Brook Farm Campground; **TO:** Webster Brook (Grand Pitch); **DISTANCE in miles (one way):** 6.5; **HIKING TIME in hours (one way):** 4; **NOTES:** Lean-to available at Grand Pitch. Excellent stream fishing in deep pools and running riffle areas.

FROM: Perimeter Road (Trout Brook Farm Area); **TO:** Lower Fowler Pond; **DISTANCE in miles (one way):** 2; **HIKING TIME in hours (one way):** 1.5; **NOTES:** Good day hike. Canoes may be rented and camping is allowed; obtain information at nearest park ranger station.

FROM: Perimeter Road (Trout Brook Farm Area); **TO:** Littlefield Pond; **DISTANCE in miles (one way):** 1.5; **HIKING TIME in hours (one way):** 1-1.5; **NOTES:** Good day hike. Canoes may be rented and camping is allowed; obtain information at nearest park ranger station.

FROM: Perimeter Road (Katahdin Stream Campground Area); **TO:** Foss and Knowlton Pond; **DISTANCE in miles (one way):** 3.5; **HIKING TIME in hours (one way):** 2-2.5; **NOTES:** Restricted to FFO. NO CAMPING OR CANOES AVAILABLE.

The following ponds are accessible only from Russell Pond Campground which is a seven-mile hike from Roaring Brook Campground. Distance given is from Russell Pond.

FROM: Russell Pond; **TO:** Six Ponds; **DISTANCE in miles (one way):** 1.7; **HIKING TIME in hours (one way):** 1.

FROM: Russell Pond; **TO:** Wassataquoik Lake; **DISTANCE in miles (one way):** 2.5; **HIKING TIME in hours (one way):** 1.5; **NOTES:** Some good fishing can be found here but, due to size of lake, weather plays an important part in success.

MT. BLUE STATE PARK AREA—WELD, MAINE

FROM: Weld Village; **TO:** Tumbledown Pond (via Parker Ridge Trail); **DISTANCE in miles (one way):** 6.7 miles (only 3 miles must be hiked, the remaining 3.7 miles may be traveled by automobile); **HIKING TIME in hours (one way):** 2.5-3; **NOTES:** NO LEAN-TOS OR CANOES AVAILABLE. Moderate climb. Good fishing late spring.

Photo by Paul Knaut, Jr.

Chapter 8
ATLANTIC SALMON FISHING

A strong, steady rain belted the Maine coast that Memorial Day weekend. Like every other stream and river from Eastport to Kittery, the Narraguagus River had swollen to almost unfishable height that weekend. But after driving 200 miles, the urge was too great—I had to wet a line.

At Stillwater Pool, the run-off water had created a powerful whirlpool, making it most difficult to work a fly properly. An hour of unproductive casting pushed me downstream to a point of land sixty yards above Cable Pool. The current was quieter there, and although I thought the heavy water flow would keep the fish down, I was hoping that luck would be with me and that a salmon would accept my offering.

The shore to my left was clear for a hundred yards. Casting across and slightly downstream, I allowed the streamer to drift with the current, finally mending it and working the Black Bear pattern upstream 10 yards from shore. No results, and the cast was repeated.

Another hour of uneventful casting passed, and the rain continued to drench the world around me. I progressed another 20 yards downstream, deciding to work my fly slightly upstream to get the full drift of the river within casting reach. On my third cast, as the offering swung from its dead drift into the current, I felt a slight nudge on the fly—so slight, in fact, that I thought little of it until I gave a jerk on the line and felt the full pulling power of the fish. I had hooked a salmon, and the battle I had been waiting for was on!

Without hesitation, the salmon broke water and headed toward the center of the river. Knowing the pull of the current and the power of the fish, I realized that if he got downstream and started to run, aided by the high water, all would be lost. Keeping my rod high, I gave the line another tug, hoping to turn the fish upstream. Instead, he broke water again. In that brief instant, awed by the sight of this magnificent fish literally standing on his tail as he moved downstream, I dropped my rod tip. With one powerful tug the line went limp, and as quick as he had come, the salmon disappeared into the river.

Seconds, minutes passed, and still the excitement refused to let me go. After nearly three hours of casting in a driving rain, I had hooked an Atlantic salmon, only to have him escape in a dramatic and powerful run downstream! I had lost the prize, but yet I was a fortunate fly fisherman—I had hooked and fought, for a few brief minutes, the most prized sport fish Maine has to offer—the Atlantic salmon, *Salmo salar*.

THE FISH

The Atlantic salmon is a belligerent battler on the end of a fly rod. His spawning characteristics, and migrations into Maine's fresh water rivers, make him a tactful and frustrating adversary. The Atlantic salmon eats little, but once he has left salt water, he will accept both dry and wet imitations if aggravated by constant casting to a specific lie, or if the angler finds him in a rare cooperative mood. Nine out of ten Atlantic salmon are hooked as a result of anger—not hunger.

Because of these traits, and his reluctance to accept a fly under ordinary circumstances, the Atlantic salmon has become a prized quarry in Maine-and wherever he is found. Challenging him requires strong, powerful equipment, and is often considered the ultimate in fly fishing. Fighting the Atlantic is unquestionably the biggest test of a fly fisherman's skill—and not all examples hooked are necessarily netted. Regardless of the efforts of the several thousand fly fishermen who seek the Atlantic salmon in Maine annually, only about 1,000 fish are actually landed.

The Atlantic salmon is an anadromous fish, spending most of its life in salt water and entering fresh water only to spawn. The life of *Salmo salar* is unique in several respects, and the natural threats, including those posed by man, are numerous. Those of us who have taken the time to study this fish respect him not only for his angling qualities, but because we realize that his battle for survival is a constant struggle from birth, and that those that have returned to fresh water are only a few of thousands.

Characteristically, Atlantic salmon start to enter Maine rivers in late May, with peak migration runs occurring in June and July. Steady movement upstream, however, is common through August and September, so angling for them during these months can be rewarding if water conditions are cooperative. Salmon entering fresh water rivers are called *bright* salmon, and fishing for them is productive throughout the season.

Spawning occurs generally in late October or early November in Maine rivers, although water levels and temperatures may delay the event. As with other species, the spawning site is called a *redd* and, when completed, may be as much as 20 feet long and three feet wide. Deposition of eggs varies depending upon the size of the female, but 800 eggs for each pound of weight of the female is not uncommon. Fecundity studies conducted by the Atlantic Sea Run Salmon Commission on the Machias and Narraguagus Rivers showed that from 3,500 to nearly 19,000 eggs may be dropped, depending upon the female's weight.

Unlike the various species of Pacific coast salmon, the Atlantic does not die after spawning, but rather lives to enter fresh water and conduct the breeding ritual several times. Specimens have been known to spawn in as many as five consecutive seasons, although salmon of this age are rare. Of the salmon caught in Maine rivers, only three to five percent are three years old, while only five to ten percent are spawning for the second or third time!

Atlantic salmon that have spawned are called *black* salmon. Generally, these spent fish return to the sea after the mating procedure has ceased, but many linger in deep, freshwater pools through the winter, returning to salt water in the spring. Having lost between 25 and 30 percent of their body weight during the winter, black salmon do not offer the famed battling resistance of bright salmon. But they can, and often will, show a reluctance to be netted. As a rule, black salmon are taken in the spring as they drift and make their way back to the sea. Most fishermen release these fish, however, for they are not as tasty as those taken during the spring or summer migration.

Salmon eggs deposited in the fall usually hatch in March, but occasionally in early April. The *alevin*, as the sac-fry are called, are between one half-inch and one inch in length, and have a yoke sac attached to their underside. When the sac is totally absorbed (when the fry are six to seven weeks old), the young leave the security of their gravel beds and enter the river.

The remain in this environment for two or three years, and are called *parr* because of a series of vertical bars along their sides; it is at this pont that Atlantic salmon parr and brown trout parr are hard to identify.

A careful eye will see the slightly forked tail, the adipose fin trimmed with red, and the spots on the dorsal fin and opercle of the brown trout—the only obvious markings distinguishing the brown from the Atlantic.

As the time nears for the parr to leave fresh water, they undergo several changes, becoming what are called *smolts*. They become thinner, the tail becomes deeply forked and elongated, and the parr marks disappear as they turn bright silver. As these young fish leave the relative safety of the river, they are from five to ten inches long. They will not return to the river of their birth for at least a year.

The mortality rate of Atlantic salmon at sea is extremely high. Smolts leaving the river are quite unprepared for the hazards facing them, and it is estimated that, for every 100 smolts that enter salt water in the spring, only one to three will survive and return as adults. They are immediate prey for a variety of birds—sea gulls, mergansers, cormorants, and others—and, as they move farther from shore, seals and larger predator fish feed on them as well. As if this were not enough, the adult salmon or yearlings must also contend with commercial fishermen along the Canadian coast—actually the Atlantic salmon's greatest predator.

Atlantic salmon entering fresh water after spending only one year at sea are known as *grilse*—while those entering after a longer sea run are called salmon. Studies of scale samples taken from Maine salmon have shown that only one or two percent of the fish entering our rivers are entering for the first time (grilse); the majority have spent two winters at sea.

The size of Maine Atlantic salmon is often said to be impressively large, yet Maine samples do not grow to the proportions of Canadian fish. The current state record taken with rod and reel is a 26 lb., 2 oz. lunker taken from the Narraguagus River in 1959. Today, fish of more than 20 pounds are uncommon. Under current conditions, the average Maine Atlantic salmon will measure between 27 and 32 inches in length, and will weigh between seven and 12 pounds; not a bad fish if you can get him on the line!

ATLANTIC SALMON GEAR

The Atlantic salmon is a powerful fish, possessing magnificent strength and stamina. Once hooked, it is not uncommon for a salmon to put up a fight lasting for a half-hour or longer. If the angler hopes to be the victor in this contest, he must utilize a rod with backbone, and line and leader capable of taking the punishment often encountered in battles with salmon.

On the majority of Maine rivers, long casts are not often needed, although a long presentation may be needed to hit certain lies at the Bangor Salmon Pool on the Penobscot. On the Narraguagus, Dennys, and Union rivers, for example, a 50-foot cast will put the fly within reach of the more productive holding areas—such is the case on the majority of Maine salmon rivers.

In these situations, I have always depended upon a rod with backbone, rather than a rod built for casting great distances. Many experienced and avid Atlantic salmon fishermen, however, prefer a rod of moderate strength, but one that has the ability to throw a fly 70 or 80 feet effortlessly, relying on their skill to bring the fish to the net. Considering that the majority of us are not avid sea run salmon fishermen, and considering the strength and power of these fish, a stiff rod with some power and backbone, rather than one designed for casting great distances, is recommended for the novice enthusiast.

The most popular rod length is nine to nine and one-half feet on Down East rivers. A *graphite* rod eight and one-half feet in length does a fine job in educated hands, but rods of shorter lengths are not recommended. A fiberglass rod should be no shorter than nine feet. Heavy lines (weights 8, 9, and 10) are generally the rule. And leaders of 10- to 12-pound test are recommended in times of high water, while 6- to 8- pound test leaders will suffice during periods of low water. Leaders are usually 8 to 12 feet in length, depending upon the fisherman and the type of fly being used—usually the longer the leader, the better.

A reel capable of holding the fly line plus at least 150 yards of 12-pound test black nylon backing is advised. Reels three and one-half to four inches in diameter, with adjustable drag, are suitable.

There is a host of productive dry and wet imitations designed exclusively for Atlantic salmon fishing. Sinking designs are effective in May, and continue to take fish throughout the season. But floating patterns only become popular once water levels recede to a point where the pools and riffle areas can be worked properly. As a rule, floating lines are used with both wet and dry flies, although lines with sinking tips may be seen in periods of high water when it is desirable to get the fly down a few extra feet. Dry flies become popular by mid-June and continue to attract salmon into July and August, losing their effectiveness in September.

If I were to select three wet fly patterns for general use on salmon in Maine rivers, I would choose the Cosseboom, the Rusty Rat, and Black Bear hair flies tied with fluorescent orange, yellow, red, and green butts. There are other productive patterns, of course, but fishing records show that these three patterns take the majority of salmon below the surface. They have certainly proven successful for me. Other productive wet flies would include the Jock

Scott, Copper Killer, Black Dose, Red Abby, Blue Charm, Durham Ranger, Mickey Finn, and Silver Rat. The Orange and Yellow Cossebooms are also productive, as are the different shades in the Rat pattern—the Black, Brown, and Gray Rats.

The Wulff design has been extremely popular in Maine in sizes 4, 6 and 8; Brown, Black, and White Wulffs are the popular choice, although the Gray, Wulff has gained in popularity. The MacIntosh is popular, as is the Pink Lady, the Brown Bivisible, the Badger Bivisible, the Irresistible, and the Rat-Faced McDougal. One of the most popular floating patterns to come along in recent years, however, is the Bomber, a clipped deer hair fly.

Much of the casting for Atlantics during the dry fly season is in areas where large, high-floating flies are required. This includes areas where the current is broken by a partly submerged boulder, creating a slight riffle, or where a rapid empties into a pool, or along the edge of rapid areas.

TECHNIQUE

There is a great difference between casting for brook trout and for Atlantic salmon. While squaretails are often disturbed by the flashing of a fly rod or by a misplaced presentation, salmon are not. I have heard experienced anglers tell of how they have actually seen the fish in his lie, disdaining the fisherman's presence. After repeated casts, the salmon still refused to strike, and his general location varied only slightly. Long, impressive casts, and remaining as inconspicuous as possible, may assist in attracting a strike. But many anglers would rather see the lie, and its occupant, and conduct a proper presentation, knowing that minute disturbances on or above the water will not affect his chances of success.

How and where we place the fly are the keys to strikes. We must remember that Atlantic salmon do not feed in fresh water—irritation is a stronger motivator than hunger. Repeatedly putting a fly close to a known salmon lie, therefore, improves chances of success, but there are certain casting techniques for the dry and sinking fly which may seem somewhat unorthodox to the trout fisherman.

Usually, the wet salmon fly is cast across and slightly downstream. Many anglers choose to fish the line loose, letting it drift naturally with the current, while others prefer to keep the line taut and under control during its complete drift. Both techniques are productive. But the most important thing is to keep the fly drifting in front of the line and leader.

Photo by Kenneth O. Allen, Jr.

Because the line and leader weigh more than the feathered and haired artificial, they are more susceptible to drag and thus often overtake the fly during the drift. The dilemma is a common one, and must be remedied by mending to keep line and leader in a curved formation above the fly.

The wet fly is most productive when fished close to the surface during normal water conditions; where water is rough or high, however, getting it down an extra foot or so can make all the difference. I prefer to fish lies which are relatively close to shore, and which are slightly shallower than the typical lie. And I have found the wet salmon fly more productive in these areas than in deeper habitat.

I like to work the sinking fly dead-drift in such a fashion that it comes to the fish either on an angle or sideways rather with its nose pointed upstream. I believe that such a delivery is the best presentation, for it has always worked best for me on Maine rivers when water levels demand a wet fly.

Although the wet salmon fly is traditionally cast across the downstream, there are times when a specific lie can only be worked directly downstream. Under such circumstances, the downstream cast cannot be helped, but can still be productive if the fly is presented properly. Under all conditions, however, the offering should be allowed to hang several moments before being retrieved and recast.

The dry salmon fly is, like the wet fly, nearly always fished across and slightly downstream, and allowed to drift with the current. The same mending of the line is important here, although it must be conducted more delicately since the fly is on the surface. Again, certain conditions require that the dry be fished directly upstream and, on occasion, downstream. The angler should not be afraid to suit the cast to the situation, as the strike often comes at the most unexpected time and in some unusual location.

THE RIVERS

At the present time, eight Maine rivers offer fishable populations of Atlantic sea run salmon. A hundred years ago, these fighting marvels were found in more than 20 rivers and large streams along the Maine coast, even as far south as Kittery. By the turn of this century, however, the construction of dams blocked migrations to major spawning grounds, and pollution and over-fishing at sea resulted in a drastic cutbacks in population, nearly extinguishing their presence entirely.

In recent years, attempts to facilitate the natural reproductive capabilities of Atlantic salmon moving into Maine rivers have met with appreciable success. Impassible dams have been altered or equipped with fishways, pollution has come under control, and new laws have been passed, many of which are international. The United States and Canada are keeping a close watch on the amount of salmon taken commercially, and stocking programs are maintained and monitored by the Atlantic Sea Run Salmon Commission. All have played a major role in rebuilding the salmon's status and are responsible in large part for the angling opportunities we enjoy today.

Fishery management personnel, knowing the importance of the Atlantic salmon as a sportfish and the increasing demand which is being imposed upon Maine rivers, have supported new regulations which restrict much of the salmon angling to fly fishing only. It is felt that, while spinning gear is legal in tidal areas, all angling for salmon in Maine, whether in fresh or salt water, will eventually be restricted to fly casting. It is by far the most popular, challenging, and rewarding method in which to seek these fish.

The Maine rivers in which Atlantic salmon are found offer a variety of angling challenges. Most are a combination of rapid and riffle areas separated by quieter stretches and deep pools. Production in upstream stretches is influenced a great deal by tides, as migrations into fresh water areas usually follow the incoming tide.

For this reason, two of the best times to try one's luck are when the tide is incoming at dawn or just before dusk, and during the two hours before and after dead high tide. At these times, the angler is working the river as fish are being pushed upstream, and as salmon enter known holding areas and lies.

The Penobscot

The Penobscot River is the largest river along the Maine coast where Atlantic salmon will be found, and is also the most productive—the catch averages close to 360 fish annually. The most popular area along the Penobscot is on the Brewer shore—the Bangor Salmon Pool. This stretch is under tidal influence, fluctuating nearly seven feet daily, which causes almost constant changes in the salmon lies. While statistics show that production is far better than other Maine rivers, this is due primarily to heavy fishing pressure. Because of the Penobscot's size, working some of the better pools and holding areas can be difficult.

Angling is sometimes conducted from boats anchored in mid-stream. Wading is also popular, but it can be dangerous because of the Penobscot's swift current. The majority of fish, however, are taken by casting from shore with long (10-foot), powerful rods capable of casting great distances.

Salmon fishing on the Narraguagus River

Action in the Penobscot can start early, but May 15 through May 20 is when things usually start rolling. Water flow is often high at this time, however, and wet flies up to size 5/0 are used to get down where resting salmon might accept them. Also, because of the powerful current, leaders up to 12- and 14-pound test are popular during the spring season.

The Narraguagus River

Maine's second largest Atlantic salmon-producing river is the Narraguagus, particularly the stretch from the town of Cherryfield to the tide mark. Because of the excellent holding pools upstream from the ice control dam at Stillwater Pool, however, the Narraguagus is also one of Maine's most versatile salmon rivers. An average of 130 fish are netted there annually, and there is every indication the Narraguagus will continue to prosper.

As with many coastal rivers, the Narraguagus was exploited by our ancestors. Log drives, forest fires, and dam construction helped in the rapid decline of the river's salmon runs, and by the mid-1870s, the annual migrations were all but non-existent. Fishways in five dams at Cherryfield just after the turn of the century helped keep a small annual migration present in the Narraguagus, however. And when the wooden dams near the rivers mouth were washed away by ice jams in 1942, salmon runs continued to improve.

By 1950, sport fishing for Atlantic salmon along the stretch of river below Cherryfield became highly popular, and in 1959, 167 salmon were taken on rod and reel, the highest number in recent years. Starting in 1962, the stocking of hatchery-reared smolts has been an annual procedure on the Narraguagus, and the investment continues to pay off in a steady production of adult salmon.

The Narraguagus has always been one of my favorite salmon rivers. It was the river where my Atlantic salmon addiction started, and I still prefer its narrowness and its enticing eddies and pools to the large width and depth of the Penobscot. For the beginner, the Narraguagus is ideal for learning the techniques of reading the water and presenting the fly. I highly recommend it.

There are at least 12 productive pools along the Narraguagus, the most popular being Cable Pool. Downstream there are the Maples, the Railroad Bridge, Stillwater, Gull Rock, Blueberry, Pumphouse, Bulldozer, Dynamo, Academy, and the Tidal Falls Pool located five miles south of Cherryfield. Action in these pools usually starts the week before Memorial Day, with wet flies taking the majority of fish. By the second week of June, however, dry flies take over and remain popular into the final days of September.

Upstream from Cable Pool, the angler will find Little Falls, Schoodic, and Deblois Bridge pools. These areas, particularly the first two, are somewhat difficult to locate but can be highly productive in the late season after salmon have moved up from the pools downstream.

The Machias and East Machias Rivers

The Machias River has the distinction of maintaining the largest self-sustaining Atlantic salmon fishery in Maine. Angling success is far short of that on the Penobscot or Narraguagus, but in 1978, 105 fish were taken on rod and reel, and the Machias has improved steadily since 1973 when all impassable dams had been either removed or equipped with fishways.

Success on the Machias fluctuates, depending a great deal upon existing water conditions. As a rule, action is possible by late May, but if high water continues longer than normal, migration upstream can be set back until middle or late June. Under such conditions, salmon have a difficult task passing through the Gorge at Machias, which greatly effects the production and the salmon's availability upstream. As with the other rivers, wet patterns start the season's action, with dry flies becoming popular later as conditions change.

The Machias has an impressive history of Atlantic salmon migrations and it is quite possible that this river experienced one of the largest runs along the Maine coast before commercial fishing nearly exhausted the fishery a century ago. An early Commissioner's report states that, "...a man with a dipnet could take 60 in a day," indicating the salmon's abundance and vulnerability before human factors resulted in their rapid decline.

Of the Atlantic salmon rivers along the Maine coast, the Machias is truly one of the most unique and challenging to anglers. Water fluctuation is constant but regulated, allowing a sufficient flow even during low-water seasons. Thus, despite current rainfall tables or weather conditions, the angler can rely on acceptable levels in the river. The Machias is the only salmon river in Maine that can assure this, and, because of this controlling ability, the productive angling season is often longer than on other Maine salmon rivers.

It is the pools along the Machias that have always interested me as a salmon fisherman. Many of the upstream areas are large, quiet pools which offer excellent possibilities with floating imitations. By the first week of June, for example, Munson is usually ready for dry fly action, while Wigwam starts to produce with floaters later on. Many of the pools along the Machias, however, are literally under-fished, with many of the local anglers concentrating on the more accessible areas near Whitneyville—the majority of fish are taken between the Gorge above Machias and Point Pool in Whitneyville. In this stretch, are Munson's Pitch, the Railroad Bridge, Boom House, and Mony Island.

There are a number of productive pools upstream. Although not as cooperative as those areas closer to the sea, the lies north of Whitneyville have become extremely popular in recent years. They experience less fishing pressure, and chances of success are improving. Some of the more popular pools are Getchell's Riffles, Wigwams, Holmes Falls, Bacon Field, Boot Rips, Little Falls, Great Falls, Carrick Pitch, and Route 9. Several areas are difficult to locate, and reach, but it's well worth the effort.

While angling opportunities are plentiful along the Machias, a different story awaits the angler on the East Machias, located four miles east of the Machias. The river for the most part is rapid and narrow, and its salmon migration is usually small and varies from year to year. Productive pools are few, the three important areas being Hydro, Berry, and Mill pools. Berry and Mill pools are excellent for the dry fly fisherman.

The Dennys River

Maine's easternmost salmon river and its fourth largest producer is the Dennys River, which enters Cobscook Bay at the town of Dennysville. Only 75 salmon were taken on rod and reel there in 1978, but this number is appreciable, considering that only 84 salmon are reported to have been taken there in 1937.

The Dennys is one of the smallest salmon rivers in Maine. It is quite narrow above Dennysville, but still offers some excellent angling opportunities. Much of the pressure is concentrated between tidal water and the confluence with Cathance Stream, although a limited number of pools and riffle areas offer some chance for success further upstream.

The heavily hit areas include the Dam Pool, the Rips, the Gut, Charlie's Rips, Lower Cathance, Fisher's Stump, Community Pool (near the mouth of Cathance Pool), and Ledge Pool. Upstream spots include Trestle and Dodge pools and The Narrows. Many of these popular lies are easily reached, particularly Charlie's Rips—one of the most productive pools. But, as is the case on the majority of Maine's salmon rivers, several good areas are difficult to find.

Because of the Dennys' size, productive salmon fishing is restricted. The majority of fish are taken from mid-May through mid-June, when water levels and cool temperature draw fish upstream. After this time, however, higher temperatures and possible low water hamper success, although an occasional salmon may be taken in the deeper pools or where riffle areas have kept the water a few degrees cooler. A late season visit, therefore, is not advised. But an attempt during the spring season may prove rewarding.

The Sheepscot

Maine's southernmost salmon river is the Sheepscot. The Sheepscot is not considered a major Atlantic salmon river, but because it does support a small population and attract a limited migration annually, it is given credit as a salmon resource.

The majority of angling is restricted to the tidal areas between Alna and Newcastle. One of the best pools is midway up the estuary at a site called Sheepscot Falls. A rock ledge creates a slight drop there, offering some productive water in late May; this area can also be productive to the end of June with dry flies. Because much of the best salmon water is influenced by tides, however, action can be received throughout the open season but with limited success. Few fish are taken from the Sheepscot annually (only 35 in 1978), with the bulk coming from the Alna/Head Tide area.

While the Sheepscot remains on the bottom of Maine's list of productive salmon rivers, there is bright hope for its future. Continued stocking and fishway construction programs since 1948 have helped the Sheepscot in its comeback attempt. And it is hoped that one to three percent of the stocked smolt will eventually return to the river annually; this represents about 300 adult salmon.

Considering the amount of fish now being taken each season on rod and reel, it is possible that the Sheepscot has surpassed this expectation and that the Atlantic salmon is now well established on annual migrations. Another important factor is that, for the first time in more than a century, spawning salmon have access to areas upstream—this definitely helps rebuild the resource.

A fact which may prove detrimental to the Sheepscot in future years, however, is its closeness to some of Maine's largest urban areas. Portland, Lewiston/Auburn, and Augusta—all are within 90 minutes drive, which, if the river becomes known as a hot salmon-producing habitat, could mean increased pressure—pressure that the river might not be able to stand.

It is quite possible that stiffer regulations will be needed on the Sheepscot because of this pressure in years ahead. But the strength of the river's comeback will determine its importance as an Atlantic salmon fishery. We can assist in this comeback by releasing all salmon landed there, a conservation tactic which I wholeheartedly support.

The Pleasant River

Ten miles east of the Narraguagus, the Pleasant River passes through the town of Columbia Falls, dumping into tidewater after plunging over Saco Falls. The Pleasant is considered one of Maine's eight most important Atlantic salmon rivers, although it produces few fish annually. Only 16 salmon were netted there in 1978, and the seasonal catch varies only slightly.

The Pleasant is not a salmon fisherman's Utopia. On the contrary, angling is quite difficult there due to a heavily forested shoreline. And because of steep dropoffs, wading is a problem as well. At several points, a succession of roll casts may raise an aggravated fish. But a fisherman traveling to this region would likely be better rewarded if his efforts were aimed toward the Narraguagus or Machias, both within relatively short distances of the Pleasant. The majority of fish here are taken by locals who fish the river below Saco Falls from a canoe or small boat.

The Union River

Like the Pleasant, the Union River stands more as a local salmon fishery than a major statewide attraction. Fewer than a dozen Atlantics have been taken there annually for the past several years, and those have been the prizes largely of local anglers. The visiting fly fisherman has a chance at success, but productive salmon water is limited.

Nearly all angling on the Union is done in tidal water below the hydroelectric dam in Ellsworth. Many of the pools and lies are under constant pressure from the fluctuation of tides and output from the dam. And, because of their location and closeness to the sea, strong spring currents keep salmon from moving upstream until mid-June. Once fish move upstream, however, it is possible to find action until the end of the season.

It is not known exactly how big a role the Union River will play in Maine's continuing effort to keep its Atlantic salmon fishery strong and flourishing. Because of the desire to keep the upper reaches of the river suitable for brook trout and brown trout, it is doubtful that strong migrations, or a self-sufficient resource, will ever be seen. At the present time, the Atlantic salmon is a popular and highly sought sportfish locally—but there is little chance that the Union will become one of Maine's leading salmon rivers.

Other Salmon Rivers

In an effort to establish the sea run Atlantic salmon in other Maine rivers, the Atlantic Sea Run Salmon Commission has been experimenting with, and testing, a number of areas along the coast as potential salmon habitats. Few rivers meet the necessary requirements, largely because of dams without proper fishway facilities, pollution, and other natural and manmade factors. But limited success has been seen in the Saco River, the St. Croix River, the Kennebec River, and, most recently, Boyden Stream. Salmon have appeared naturally in several smaller tributary waters of major rivers, like Kenduskeag Stream on the Penobscot and Bond Brook on the Kennebec.

The value of these rivers as Atlantic salmon angling areas is limited, to say the least. Continued stocking efforts, the building of fishways, proper management, and cleansing of the water, however, may see increased migrations in years ahead.

SUMMARY

Penobscot River — Best times — mid-May; June; September through mid-October. Productive flies — wet: Cosseboom, Mickey Finn, Jock Scott, Durham Ranger, Blue Charm, Silver Wilkinson; dry: Bomber, Grey Wulff, Brown Bivisible, MacIntosh. Productive areas — Bangor Salmon Pool

Narraguagus River — Best times — week before Labor Day to end of June; September to October 15. Productive flies—wet: Black Bear, Cosseboom, Rusty Rat, Blue Charm; dry: Bomber, all Wullfs, Brown Bivisible, Rat-Faced McDougal. Productive areas — Cable Pool, Stillwater, Railroad Bridge.

Machias River — Best times — depend upon water flow; late May through June are prime; September through October 15. Productive flies — wet: Cosseboom, Mickey Finn, Rusty Rat, Blue Charm; dry: Bomber, White/Brown Wulffs, Brown Bivisible, Pink Lady Palmer. Productive areas—Munson Pitch, Wigwams, Railroad Bridge.

East Machias River — Best times — mid-May to mid-June, perhaps into early July. Productive flies — wet: Coseboom, Rusty Rat, Blue Charm; dry: Bomber, Pink Lady Palmer, Brown Wulff. Productive areas — Hydro Pool, Berry Pool, Mill Pool.

Dennys River — Best times — mid-May through mid-June; possibly fall if water levels permit. Productive flies — wet: Squirrel Tail, Cosseboom, Black Bear, Mickey Finn, Jock Scott; dry: Bomber, Pink Lady Palmer, all Wulffs. Productive areas — Charlie's Rips, Dam Pool, Community Pool.

Sheepscot River — Best times — mid-May through June. Productive flies — wet: Cosseboom, Black Bear, Blue Charm, Mickey Finn; dry: Bomber, all Wulffs, Brown Bivisible, Pink Lady Palmer. Productive areas — Head Tide Dam, Sheepscot Falls.

Pleasant River — Best times — mid-May through June; perhaps September and early October, depending upon water levels. Productive flies — wet: Blue Charm, Cosseboom, Black Bear, Jock Scott; dry: Bomber, all Wulffs. Productive areas — below Saco Falls.

Union River — Best times — early or mid-June through October 15. Productive flies — wet: Orange Blossom, Black Bear, (orange Butt), Cosseboom, Mickey Finn. Dry: Bomber, Pink Lady Palmer. Productive areas — below hydro dam at Ellsworth.

NOTE: Other productive wet flies which should be carried include the Copper Killer, Shrimp, Black Spider, Yellow Butt Black Bear, Thunder and Lightning, Black Bomber, Black Doze, sizes 4 and 8.

Chapter 9
A WORD ON EQUIPMENT

The equipment which a fly fisherman utilizes is highly important and should be selected with great care to fill specific needs. The rod, reel, line, and leader are considered basic requirements, and there are other tools which can make our sport both easier and more enjoyable.

In this chapter, we will look at the different rod types and lengths, reels, line tapers, and leader elements, and determine which are best for the majority of Maine conditions. We will also look at some other equipment synonymous with the fly fishing fraternity, discover its contributions and determine whether it is needed, or beneficial in our sport. I hope that, once we are finished, you will know what is needed for equipment and (with the list of retail outlets furnished at the end of the chapter) know where you can do business while traveling through Maine.

RODS

Today's fly fisherman has available the finest fly rods ever made. Never before has the angler had such a selection to choose from—such a variation of materials, lengths, actions, and weights. Selecting a fly rod today is as simple as learning the basic casting fundamentals once we know what we want.

149

There are basically three materials from which modern fly rods are made; bamboo, fiberglass, and graphite. Bamboo rods are quite expensive and relatively delicate and are not the rods with which one would want to bushwhack through the Maine woods. They are, in the minds of many fly fishermen, the best casting tool money can buy, however.

I believe that the best rod for an angler is the one which fits, and feels right for, that individual. Too much has already been said about which rod material is best; the truth is, all three are excellent, particularly when manufactured under today's standards—but only in the hands of the right caster. Remember—if a fisherman buys a graphite rod, it doesn't necessarily mean he will outcast or outfish the fiberglass enthusiast. The rod that fits the hand and feels comfortable is the best casting instrument money can buy, regardless of price *or* material.

The fiberglass rod is the most popular one on the market today. This is due largely to the attractive price, and to the fact that fiberglass has become the standard material of American fishing poles and fly rods. I believe that graphite will eventually overtake and pass fiberglass in popularity, but glass rods presently dominate the market, and undoubtedly will for the next few years.

A good fiberglass fly rod is not expensive—this is one factor which keeps this material on top of the popularity list. For between $20 and $35, the fisherman can obtain an excellent rod capable of filling any requirement in Maine, except Atlantic salmon fishing. Another $20 would enable one to purchase one of the best fiberglass rods on the market, one which would unquestionably fit all the caster's needs and make his efforts more enjoyable.

Fiberglass rods offer several characteristics (besides price) which have added to their popularity. The basic glass rod is strong and durable to withstand the abuse often encountered in the field. Its elasticity, long life and versatility often outclass many bamboo rods, making this a smart investment for the average fly fisherman. Although the fiberglass rod does not exhibit the delicate response of bamboo or graphite, the fisherman will discover that this sensitivity is not always required under Maine conditions. I would say that the fiberglass rod is the best instrument for the novice enthusiast, and I would recommend it for all practical purposes.

Since their introduction in the early 1970s, rods made of boron and high modulous graphite have taken the American fly fishing fraternity by storm. Not only are these instruments 25 to 30 percent lighter than comparable fiberglass rods, but they possess nearly double the strength as well. I personally use a graphite rod, and seldom use any other. Graphite rods are expensive, however, priced between $80 and $150.

For the purist, however, graphite rods are a lifesaver. Their ability to lift the line from the water is phenomenal, and their delicate response to the caster's wishes makes them a joy to use. Because of these rods' power and elasticity, the caster will soon discover that he can present more line—and control it better—than with a glass rod. And the lightweight characteristic of graphite allows accurate presentations for a longer period of time than any other material available.

Rod length is often a controversial topic among fly fishermen and it's doubtful that the debate will ever be settled. The most popular rod lengths in Maine are 8 and 8½ feet, and I would agree that both are practical here. The majority of fiberglass rods seem to be of the 8½-foot caliber, but an 8-foot graphite rod will cover any situation confronted; the difference in lengths is due to the variations in power of the two materials.

Rods shorter than eight feet are not necessary under the majority of Maine conditions. I own a seven-foot, two-piece fiberglass rod which I use primarily during the early season on small brooks and streams, but it rarely leaves its case throughout the remainder of the season.

On the West Branch of the Penobscot, a short rod would be detrimental to an angler's casting ability to place the fly in hard-to-reach lies. Unless the fisherman is an expert rod handler, this would be the case on most of Maine's important and productive salmon rivers. I have found that short fly rods are characteristically more difficult to work with than longer ones; they are either too stiff or too limber—no happy medium. Even while fishing smaller trout habitats such as Nesowadnehunk Stream or Spencer Stream in Somerset County, short rods can greatly restrict the angler's delivery and casting ability, thus affecting his productivity.

The action of a fly rod depends greatly upon the individual, but rods with a stiff action are easier to work with under most conditions. Experienced casters, or those wanting long, delicate, and impressive deliveries, may choose a more limber stick. But the two-piece, stiffer rods are more popular.

An easy, although not precise method of determining a rod's action, is to gently place the rod in the palm of the hand with the tip on the floor. If the first 15 to 18 inches bend with no pressure applied, there's a good chance that the rod is fast, or strong-actioned. If the bend extends to the mid-section, it is a medium-action rod, and if the curve meets the handle, it is a slow-action rod.

Modern fly rods are designed and built to handle specific line weights. The better sticks are marked near the handle with the AFTMA (American Fishing Tackle Manufacturers' Association) line weight recommendation—so selection of the proper line for a rod is not a difficult chore.

If, for example, a rod is marked "856", that rod is 8½ feet long and takes a number 6 line. If it is marked "8056", it is 8 feet long and can handle either a number 5 or number 6 line effectively. Many rods have the recommended line weight written simply "AFTMA Fly Line No. 6".

When purchasing a fly rod, the angler should consider the type of habitat he will be fishing. If remote trout ponds, or medium-sized streams and rivers with moderate current, are goals, a rod designed for number 5 line would be a good choice. On the other hand, if rivers such as the West Branch of the Penobscot, the Moose, and the Rapid were to be principal targets, a slightly heavier line would be needed (a rod to accommodate a number 6 would be suitable). This rod-and-line combination would also be good for black bass fishing in all types of habitat.

Small streams composed of deadwater areas and deep pools, and beaver flowages, could be worked effectively with a number 4 line—rarely will a line smaller than this be required in Maine. Considering the habitat Maine has to offer the fly fisherman, either a number 5 or number 6 line would be a good selection for general use.

Below is a list of line weights recommended for specific habitats.

TYPE OF HABITAT	RECOMMENDED LINE WEIGHT
Calm streams, medium-sized brooks, beaver flowages—moderate current areas	AFTMA Line No. 4
Remote trout ponds, medium-sized streams, and small rivers with strong current.	AFTMA Line No. 5 or 6
Black bass fishing in most habitats	AFTMA Line No. 6
Atlantic salmon fishing	AFTMA Line No. 8, 9, or 10

Generally speaking, the more guides on a fly rod, the better. I have an 8½-foot graphite supporting nine guides, and this is, in my opinion, the minimum; this is the standard number found on 8½-foot rods. Eight-foot rods usually carry one guide less, and the number decreases as the stick gets shorter. A seven foot rod I bought a number of years ago carries only seven guides, but a 12-inch span between guides allows too much slack in the line. On a good rod, an 8- or 9-inch separation between guides is standard. On my favorite rod, the distance between guides is roughly 8½ inches.

REELS

The fly reel has one of the easiest chores of all fly fishing equipment. Its principal job is to *house* the fly line and backing—other than an occasional battle with a huge fish, it is hardly ever used to *retrieve*. Good reels are expensive, however, and are important in balancing the fly rod—in that respect, they serve a vital purpose.

Although, under most circumstances, the fly reel is not used to fight or hold our quarry, reels with adjustable drag are recommended. On such rivers as the Rapid, where white water and strong current are common, and aid the salmon in his escape, it is often necessary to use the reel to control and turn the fish as he makes his run downstream. This is also true while fishing deep pools with powerful undertows or places with rapid areas.

The majority of fly fishing reels today are designed to accompany interchangeable spools; this is not only practical but economical, considering the prices of reels. One spool can carry floating line, while the other carries a sinking line, thus preparing the angler for both situations at a substantial savings.

FLY LINES

The fly line is one of the most important components of a fly fisherman's duffle. Because the line often has a great deal to do with the way the fly performs on or below the surface, and because it assists greatly in the presentation itself, only high-quality fly lines should be purchased. Money spent on a cheap line is money wasted, since inexpensive lines will create more problems than they are worth.

There are two basic types of fly lines: *floating* and *sinking*. And, unless a fisherman plans to be a purist with floating imitations or one of the sinking designs, he will need one fly line in each category. There are, however, some fly fishermen who utilize a dry fly line with sinking imitations, and in certain circumstances, this works very well. But when fish are deep in the spring holes during warm weather, a sinking fly line is often the only way to reach them.

All fly lines are available in several different *tapers*, the four most popular being: *double, weight forward, shooting,* and *level*, respectively. For general use in Maine, either double or weight forward taper is an excellent selection, and the actual purchase should be based largely on personal preference.

Double-tapered lines are somewhat cheaper (actually being two lines in one), and offer better delivery characteristics than any other fly line taper.

Weight forward lines, on the other hand, assist the caster in getting his fly to greater distances with less effort, and this is important on many of the larger rivers and trout ponds. Where one taper fails, the other fills the gap.

Sinking fly lines are important utensils during the early fishing season when streamers and wet flies are used in riffle areas, or when the need arises to get the offering down where fish can see it. The sinking line is equally as important to the nymph fisherman, or an angler working bucktails and small streamers close to the bottom when surface temperatures force game fish to cooler depths.

Twenty years ago, sinking fly lines were simply 30 or 35 yards of fishing line that sank below the surface of the water. But, since their introduction a decade or so ago, *sinking tip lines* have become increasingly popular, particularly since they have become available in a variety of sinking speeds. On the majority of Maine salmon and trout rivers, lines with sinking tips outnumber standard wet lines substantially, and their popularity continues to grow as more and more fishermen discover their functional and cooperative qualities.

Basically, a sinking tip line is a floating fly line with the first ten feet engineered to sink. This sinking section is a standard length on the majority of popular brand name lines, but may extend to twenty feet on "extra fast" tips. Like regular floating fly lines, sinking tips are available in a variety of weights to fit all rods, but are usually available in double and weight forward tapers only.

The contributions a sinking tip makes to the wet fly fisherman are obvious, but in order to appreciate them, these lines must be used in the field. For the nymph enthusiast, the floating portion of the line can act as a strike indicator, and even for the streamer fly fisherman, it is easier to keep track of the imitation's location by watching the section of line on top of the water.

One of the qualities I like about the floating/sinking combination is that it allows opportunity for a quick and easy lift from the water. These combination lines are almost always easier to manipulate than regular sinking lines.

LEADERS

Of all gear carried and used by the fly fisherman, the leader is the tool most often taken for granted, or given the least amount of consideration. Casters will debate for hours about the best floating imitation to represent a May fly on a remote trout pond, or about which fly line weight is most suitable for medium-sized streams. Yet, when it comes to leaders, fishermen are usually uninterested in, or reluctant to, talk about it.

This is unfortunate, for the proper leader can boost productivity by as much as 50 percent—particularly when working habitats where the fish have clear and unobstructed visibility.

The leader's primary role is to reduce the visible connection between fly and line to give the imitation maximum appearance of freedom. For this reason, the smaller the leader (at its connecting point with the fly), the better. Contrary to popular belief, monofilament line *can* be seen to a certain degree by fish.

Leaders that taper to a fine tippet are the most popular with selective fly fishermen. Not only do they offer a fine connecting end, but they are easier to work with than level leaders in all situations except trolling. For the dry fly enthusiast, the tapered leader is a must for proper delivery, flotation, and (in streams) proper drift.

While wet fly users may insist that tapered leaders are not required below the surface, I am not convinced that this is true. Trout and salmon have been known to hit knots in leaders resting on the surface, indicating that monofilament is not as invisible to fish as many believe. Also, because a fish views the river bottom facing upstream most of the time, his "window" is horizontal and upward; monofilament has high light-refracting properties—it makes sense, therefore, that the trout can see the line above him as it approaches.

It may be said at this point that, if trout can see level leaders underwater, then tapered leaders must be seen as well; but this is not the point. The important thing is to offer as little leader visibility as possible. Leaders with tapered tippets restrict this visibility while offering flexibility for proper casting and the strength needed to bring the prize to the net.

The majority of leaders used by fly fishermen today are commercially made. Some purists insist on tying their own, but such pains need not necessarily be taken to find action. Those found in local tackle shops offer the qualities needed for proper delivery and drift, and come in a variety of length and tippet sizes. For less than $1 the caster can purchase a quality tapered leader capable of filling any demand.

The question of which leader length is best can only be answered by personal preference; each angler must choose his most effective leader length. There are certain basic guidelines I have found helpful in leader length selection, however.

If, for example, I plan on fishing for landlocked salmon with dry flies on the West Branch of the Penobscot, a leader nine feet in length with at least a 5X tippet would be required (a leader with a tippet roughly .006 inches in diameter and in the two-pound test category). On the other hand, if a river such as the Rapid was my target water—a river with white water and rough

Photo by Kenneth O. Allen, Jr.

Casting for Kennebago Lake brook trout

current—a slightly shorter leader with a stronger tippet would be utilized (an eight-footer with a 4X or two-and-one-half-pound test tippet would be sufficient). A good rule of thumb is: leaders with stronger tippets are better for rough water areas when using floating flies, while smaller tippets will cover the situation in quieter water.

With wet flies, streamers, and bucktails, however, sticking to a standard length leader and tippet size will cover most problems. The nymph fisherman may wish to vary tippet diameter according to the size of the fly.

On most Maine rivers, an eight- or nine-foot leader with a 4X (.007-inch, two-and-one-half-pound test) or 5X (.006-inch, two-pound test) is sufficient. In some of the smaller habitats a 6X leader is fine, but this is one-and-three-quarter-pound test tippet can not be bullied, and will not take the punishment, of the two larger sizes.

Below is a chart indicating leader lengths, tippet weights, and diameters for different types of habitat. These recommendations are not absolute—your personal choice may vary from those given. They have, however, worked well for me over much of the state, and are good starting points for the novice angler.

TYPE OF HABITAT	LEADER LENGTH	TIPPET DIA.	POUND TEST
Rough Water/ Strong Current	8-9 ft.	4X (.007″)	2.5
		5X (.006″)	2
Calm Water/ Medium Current	9 ft.	5X (.006″) or	2
		6X (.005″)	1.75
Small Trout Ponds, Beaver Flowages, etc.	9 ft.	6X (.005″)	1.75
Quiet, Shallow Streams	9 ft.	6X (.005″)	1.75

LEADERS FOR WET FLIES, STREAMERS, AND BUCKTAILS

TYPE OF HABITAT	LEADER LENGTH	TIPPET DIA.	POUND TEST
Most Waters	8-9 ft.	4X (.007″)	2.5
Quiet Stretches	8-9 ft.	6X (.005″)	1.75

VESTS

The fishing vest is one of the fly fisherman's most important assets, particularly to the angler who works streams and rivers away from his automobile. It is not nearly as important to the fisherman working from a canoe or boat, but to the in-stream fisherman, it is his cache, keeping his necessary gear within easy reach.

A good vest should have enough pockets to carry an assortment of dry and wet flies, leaders, fly dope, and other basic needs; and feel comfortable while allowing the fisherman free movement and casting ability. Most of the vests on the market, many sold in tackle shops, meet these requirements and are relatively inexpensive.

Some of the better vests, however, may cost as much as $40. But usually, for a cost of $15 to $20, an excellent vest can be purchased. This would probably feature eight to twelve pockets with either snap or zipper closings, and would be made of good quality poplin or cotton. More expensive vests, as a rule, have nothing more to offer except the trade name and perhaps a few more pockets, and are an extravagance for the average fisherman.

WADERS

Waders to a stream fisherman are like tools to a carpenter; he cannot do the job properly without them. To the stream enthusiast, chest waders are a necessity which allow him to maneuver into proper casting position. This in itself makes waders invaluable. The fact that chest waders also permit the caster to bend or settle in the water, obscuring his view from the fish, only increases their value and preference over hip boots.

While owning a pair of waders is a key to success for the stream fisherman, it is also an invitation to forget the dangers of wading in rivers with strong current or deep pools and dropoffs. Safety is imperative when fly fishing. This is another reason that study of a stream is vital before fishing it.

It should be remembered that walking in water is not the same as walking on land. Do not *step* while in waders, but *slide* your feet small distances along the bottom keeping your weight on your back foot until you know that the bottom ahead of you is solid. Also, when wading, upstream or down, it is best to *quarter* either against or with the current; it is much easier than trying to fight the full force. This also will help you to see the bottom, which is often obscured from view. A wading stick is a great help, not only to maintain balance but to "scout" the bottom in front of you for dropoffs and submerged rocks.

Most waders are constructed of rubber. Some of the expensive designs are made of nylon, coated with rubber on the outside and neoprene on the inside. Such waders are becoming more and more popular on most streams. Nylon-coated waders are generally lighter, easier to work with, and resistant to the rough treatment often necessary to reach secluded lies. All-rubber waders are hot and confining, and tear, or wear out at the seams, quite readily. Although less expensive, the fisherman will spend more money in the long run on rubber waders than on those made of nylon, considering repair jobs or replacement costs.

On some Maine rivers, waders are not needed to get a fly to where it might entice a fish to strike. But in the majority of cases, the angler's chances of success are greater if waders are utilized.

On the Rapid River's Middle Dam Pool, for example, it is possible, and usually more productive, to fish close to the rocks and boulders 10 to 20 feet from shore. There is ample casting room here, and in a situation like this, waders would be unnecessary for success.

A mile downstream, however, where brush overhangs the banks of Chub Pool, casting room is restricted. There, waders are important and helpful in getting a floating fly upstream for proper drift. Such diversity is common on Maine rivers and streams. I would say that, on 95 percent of the productive salmon and trout waters, chest waders would greatly improve the caster's chances for success.

LANDING NETS

Ninety percent of the fish I catch, I release. And although I am careful in my releasing techniques, a landing net is helpful in assuring the trout's safety. Many of us become excited when fighting a salmon or trout; and we should, for that is what fishing is all about.

But in the excitement, it is not difficult to internally damage a fish in an attempt to remove the fly. It has been my experience that once a fish is in a net, he is easier to handle; it is often possible to remove the fly without touching the fish at all, which again helps assure his release unharmed.

For this reason, I carry a net to the stream, and am rarely without it while fishing. Besides assisting in protecting the fishery, a landing net is very helpful in retaining large fish in fast current.

Personally, I like a deep net with a large opening and strong mesh. A bow roughly 8½ inches wide by 13½ long is good; a net 19 inches deep will hold large, powerful salmon, as well as an average-size trout. A landing net should be light for easy handling, yet strong enough to hold powerful fish.

The best landing nets are made of wood—ash bows with adjoining cherry, mahogany, or walnut handles. Such examples can be expensive, sometimes as high as $35. But, for about half that price, a good wooden net can be purchased at a number of the better tackle stores. In recent years, nets made with a metal bow and plastic handle have been flooding the market. It is true that their prices are attractive, but the nets I have seen are too light to handle large salmon or trout.

FLY BOXES

A wide variety of fly boxes is available to the fly fisherman—basically, one is as good as the other. When I first started out in this sport, I usually followed the crowd and relied on the metal boxes. But time and experience showed that many of the aluminum boxes are costly and extravagant. For about half the price, sufficient boxes molded of plastic or polypropylene can be purchased—they do the job very well. These boxes house all styles of flies, but are particularly useful for small wet imitations and streamers.

Because of the fragile construction of many dry flies (and a tendency for the hackle to mat down if overcrowded), I like to carry my floating patterns in clear plastic boxes which offer a separate compartment for each fly. When carried like this in my vest, I know the flies are not being squashed, and, because of the transparent plastic, identification can be made rapidly before opening the box. As many fly fishermen will tell you, this can be important on windswept days.

Large streamers, particularly trolling patterns, are best carried in leather bound "books" with either felt or lambswool protective pages. It is important to keep trolling flies flat and in proper shape and these books do the job nicely.

FLY DRESSING

When fishing with most varieties of dry flies, it is important to keep the imitation floating high. Therefore, to give your patterns buoyancy and long life on the surface, they must be treated to repel water. Years ago, it was quite a chore to maintain a fly's floating characteristics. But today, with the number of commercially manufactured dressing available, it is a relatively easy job.

Modern dry fly dressings come in four forms: spray, liquid, powder, and paste. Aerosol floatants work extremely well, but much is wasted in each application. Powdered dressings are excellent for flies already put through their paces once or twice but, for best results, imitations fresh from the box should be moistened before application of dressing.

The two best forms of dressing, I believe are paste and liquid. I've used the liquid silicone type for a number of years and one half-ounce bottle will last nearly a whole season; it really goes a long way and does an excellent job of impregnating a fly for high flotation.

Paste dressings are extremely popular, and when liquid applicants are not available I'll rely on one of these preparations. Each rod company and/or tackle manufacturer is now producing the "best paste dressing," but in comparing the brand names, I've found little difference; they are all effective. One advantage to paste dressings over all the others is that it takes very little to keep a fly afloat—and they are colorless, odorless, and environmentally safe.

SUN GLASSES

On bright, sunny days, productive tactics are often hampered by bothersome glare from the water's surface. Floating imitations are often lost in the sun's reflection, limiting the chances of successful setting of the hook.

A good pair of sun glasses will help solve this dilemma by cutting down the glare and cutting out other environmental factors invading the fisherman's eyesight.

Also, by reducing the glare from the surface, sun glasses offer the fisherman a better view of the stream's bottom. If working a dry fly downstream against the sun, the caster will be better able to see the best lies and holding areas where fish are apt to be if he "wears his shades."

WHERE TO GET IT

Below is a list of retail outlets located throughout the state of Maine where fly
fishing supplies may be obtained. Those preceded by an asterisk offer catalogs
and mail order deliveries.

Bedell's Tackle Shop
Skowhegan, ME 04976
(207) 474-8939

Bibeau's Fly Shop
Route 302
No. Windham, ME 04062
(207) 892-4206

Bob Leeman's Trout Shop
807 Wilson St.
Brewer, ME 04412
(207) 989-4060

Butch's Fly Shop
714 Water St.
Gardiner, ME 04345
(207) 582-3790

*Charlie's Log Cabin
Oakland, ME 04963
(207)465-2451

Eagle Sports Shop
Wilton, ME 04294
(207) 645-2500

*Eddie's Flies and Tackle
303 Broadway
Bangor, ME 04401
(207) 945-5587

Fly's, Inc.
Farmington, ME 04938
(207) 778-4885

*Joe's Tackle Shop
Rt. 1
Danforth, ME 04424
(207) 448-2909

Kittery Trading Post
Rt. 1
Kittery, ME 03904
(207) 439-2700

*L.L. Bean, Inc.
Freeport, ME 04032

Madawaska Sport Shop, Inc.
482 Main St.
Madawaska, ME 04756
(207) 728-4545

Mel's Sports
124 Main St.
Freeport Maine 04033
(207) 865-3277

Pierce's Store
Elm St.reet
Guilford, ME 04443
(207) 876-4486

Sebago Fly Shop
Rt. 113
Steep Falls, ME 04085
(207) 642-4489

Sportsman's Exchange
72 Main St.
Bridgton, ME 04009
(207) 647-3763

Woodman's Sporting Goods
223 Main St.
Norway, ME 04268
(207) 743-6602

Playing a brookie in Jones Brook, Somerville

Photo by Kenneth O. Allen, Jr.

GLOSSARY

A

abdomen - the body section of a natural or imitation nymph. Usually made of dubbing (on imitations), it covers up to two-thirds of the hook.

alder fly - a member of the genus *Sialis* which resembles the caddis fly, but lacks the wing hairs characteristic of the adult caddis. A popular trout and salmon food when other important naturals are not available, the alder fly is not considered highly important in Maine, but is still a good imitation in size 12 or 14.

anadromous - any fish which migrates from salt water into fresh water to spawn.

Atlantic salmon *(Salmo salar)* - One of the most prized and sought-after anadromous fish. Found in a selected number of Maine rivers, they enter fresh water sometime in May, spawning in the fall. Weights average between six and 10 pounds—*Salmo salar* is a mighty battler on either wet or dry flies.

attractor - a brightly colored fly which resembles no specific natural food. It is usually tied with bright feathers or bucktail, with a body of tinsel. Popular examples include the Mickey Finn, the Royal Coachman, and the Warden's Worry.

B

backcast - the motion in casting when the flyline is extended to the rear of the fly fisherman. It is an important key to proper casting technique.

bivisible - a dry fly pattern tied with hackle fibers along its entire body to offer buoyancy and visibility. Usually effective in fast and rough water, it is almost always tied with a white hackle near the eye of the hook for visibility. Popular patterns are the Brown Bivisible, Badger Bivisible, Grizzly Bivisible, and Blue Dun Bivisible.

blueback trout - a member of the genus *Salvelinus*, once common in the Rangeley Lake area of Maine; now found in less than a dozen secluded ponds in northern Maine. An inhabitant of deep, cold water, the blueback is of little importance to the fly fisherman.

body - the part of a fly tied along the shank of the hook to resemble the body of a forage fish or insect. Composed of a variety of materials (tinsel, wool, dubbing, etc.) depending upon style of fly.

bronzeback - an angling term referring to members of the bass family, particularly the smallmouth.

brookie - a term used to describe the brook trout, this is a particularly popular nickname in Maine.

bucktail - a wet fly pattern with wings composed primarily of tail hair from a deer. Popular examples are the Black Nose Dace, the Dark Edson Tiger, and the Red and White.

C

caddis fly - one of the most important natural food supplied of salmon and trout. Well established throughout Maine, they are particularly abundant on the rivers, streams, and ponds in the Rangeley Lake area. Hatching takes place predominantly in early spring through mid-summer. Popular imitations include the Adams, the White Moth, and the Male and Female Grannom in sizes 12 and 14. The Henryville Special, the Fluttering Caddis, and the Quill Wing Caddis are good imitations as well.

char - a genus of the salmonid family, of which the brook trout and lake trout are members.

covert - a term used to describe the wing case on nymphs.

crane fly - a member of the family *Tipulidae* resembling a large mosquito. Not considered an important trout or salmon food; productive imitations are few.

creel - an accessory of the fisherman in which fish are stored or carried while afield. The most common creels are made of willow, but canvas creels are now popular.

D

delta-wing - a style of downwing dry fly.

divided-wing - a style of downwing fly which resembles the wing found on the May fly. Patterns often tied in this style include the Quill Gordon, the March Brown, the Blue Dun, and the Light Cahill. This is the most used style of dry flies.

downwing - a style of fly with wings resting along its body. Popular examples include grasshoppers flies.

dressing - a solution often used to treat fly lines and flies to help them float *or* sink, depending upon their intended use.

dry fly - an imitation of a natural insect, usually in its adult state, which floats on the surface of the water.

dubbing - the fur material often used on the body section of flies. This often comes from fox and muskrats.

dun - an adult May fly, so called immediately after leaving its nymphal stage. Also called **subimago** by professional entomologists.

E

emerger - an insect changing from nymph or pupa to the adult stage. Often used when referring to May flies and caddis flies.

entomology - the study of insects and their lives, this often becomes a part of the fly fisherman's sport.

F

fanwing - a style of dry fly with wings constructed of the fan-shaped breast feathers from a wood duck. Such a formation allows light and delicate presentation to the water's surface. The most famous fanwing dry fly is the Fan-Wing Royal Coachman.

ferrule - the point at which the two portions of a fly rod connect; usually a metal or fiberglass socket and matching plug.

floating line - a line designed to float on the surface of the water, used with dry flies.

fly - copy of a natural insect, tied on a hook and composed of fur, feathers, wool, etc.

G

gnat - a member of the order *Diptera* found primarily on still ponds and large pools. Although not considered an important or vital trout food, the gnat is often essential for deceiving trout when they are feeding selectively. A popular imitation is the Black Gnat.

graphite - a high modulous material possessing great strength, 25 to 30 times lighter than fiberglass. Graphite is durable and extremely powerful, and will eventually replace fiberglass as the most common fly rod building material.

guides - the metal or oxide devices fastened to a fly rod, through which the fly line travels.

H

hackle - the part of a fly, particularly a dry fly, composed of a feather, which keeps the fly afloat.

hairwing - a style of fly with wing largely or solely composed of hair.

I

imago - the scientific term for the stage of May fly after it leaves the dun stage and has mated—the final stage of a May fly before it becomes a spinner.

Irresistible - a dry fly with body of clipped deer hair, and thick hackle and tail. An excellent floater in rough water.

L

larvae - The first stage of an insect such as the caddis fly, which has a complete life cycle.

lateral Line - A series of pores on the side of a fish, through which vibrations are absorbed—the primary hearing organ of a fish.

leader - The monofilament line separating fly line and fly.

M

May fly - an order of insects having an incomplete life cycle; eggs, nymph, and adult of significant importance to the fly fisherman.

midge - A small two-winged member of the order *Diptera* represented by a number of small imitations in sizes 18 through 22. Highly productive for trout and salmon when other important forage insects are scarce.

N

nymph - the immature aquatic stage of an insect having an imcomplete life cycle; also an imitative wet fly. Larvae and nymphs are very similar, the only difference being that the nymph has sprouted rudimentary wings.

P

parachute - a style of applying hackle to a dry fly, in which hackle is fastened to the base of an upright hairwing but parallel to the hook. An excellent floater with good buoyancy, available in any pattern. Popular patterns include the Adams and the Light Cahill.

pupa - the second stage of life of insects having a complete life cycle.

R

reduced fly - a fly which has been made smaller by omitting nonessential materials.

retrieve - the action of pulling back a fly once it has reached its zenith downstream.

S

sedge - the angling term for an adult caddis fly.

sinking line a line that is engineered to sink—used with wet flies, streamers, and nymphs.

spentwing - a downing dry fly designed to imitate a May fly or other insect that has mated and come to rest on the water.

spider - a imitative fly largely composed of sparse hackle on number 16 through 20 hooks. Tied to represent delicate insects such as spiders; also called **variant**.

spinner - the last stage of an adult May fly, after it has mated. See **imago**.

stone fly - a large member of the order *Plecopreta* of great importance to the fly fisherman. The May fly, caddis fly and stone fly are considered the "Big Three" of natural insect feed for trout and salmon. Both nymph and adult stages are represented by imitations.

streamer - a wet fly usually tied with feathers and tinsel, the most popular patterns resembling important forage fish. The Gray Ghost and Black Ghost are popular examples.

T

tag - a winding of silk, wool, etc. at the end of the body on some flies.

tandem - a fly, usually a streamer, possessing more than one hook.

terrestrial - a style of fly tied to imitate a land-based insect. Popular examples are grasshoppers, ants,and bettles.

thorax - The front third section of a nymph.

tippet - The last few inches of a tapered leader.

V

variant - see spider.

W

wet fly - a traditional fly style designed to sink in the water. Often resembles an important forage fish or insect.

APPENDIX

SOURCES OF INFORMATION

When I first started writing this book, it became apparent that there was much general information about Maine which would be of great importance to the fly fisherman. I have tried to cover as much territory as possible within the covers of this publication. But certain areas have been omitted or left out in order to dedicate as much space as possible to the more important and helpful information having a direct impact on our sport.

This book would not be complete, however, without making an attempt to supply the addresses of informational outlets. Within the following pages, therefore, are the addresses of major chambers of commerce in important fly fishing regions, as well as addresses which might assist the camper, hiker, and fisherman in obtaining factual and updated information about a specific region, or information on a statewide scale.

Also included in this chapter are the addresses of major fishing and sportsmen's clubs such as Trout Unlimited, Maine Basscasters and the Sportsman's Alliance of Maine.

CHAMBERS OF COMMERCE

The following is a list of chambers of commerce in major fishing towns. These offices supply updated local information concerning hotels, motels, sporting camps, restaurants, tackle shops, and campgrounds, and often supply the names, addresses, and telephone numbers of registered Maine guides within their regions.

Many are open only on a seasonal schedule, however, usually from June 1 through either September 30 or October 31.

Windham Chamber of Commerce
North Windham, ME 04062
Telephone (207) 892-8265

For information concerning the greater Sebago Lake area.

Rangeley Lakes Chamber of Commerce
Box 317
Rangeley, ME 04970
Telephone (207)864-5571

For information concerning the greater Rangeley Lake area.

Bingham Chamber of Commerce
Box 491
Bingham, ME 04920
Telephone (207) 672-3978

For information concerning the Kennebec River region from Bingham north to The West Forks and Indian Pond.

Jackman Chamber of Commerce
Box 496
Jackman, ME 04945
Telephone (207) 668-7628

For information concerning the Jackman area.

Greenville Chamber of Commerce
Box 581
Greenville, ME 04441
Telephone (207) 695-2702

For information concerning the greater Moosehead Lake region.

Millinocket Chamber of Commerce
Box 5
Millinocket, ME 04462
Telephone (207) 723-4443

For information concerning areas around Baxter State Park and along the West Branch of the Penobscot River up to Ripogenus Dam.

Bangor Chamber of Commerce
55 Washington St.
Bangor, ME 04401
Telephone (207) 947-0307

For information concerning the greater Bangor area.

Houlton Chamber of Commerce
109 Main St.
Houlton, ME 04730
Telephone (207) 532-3050

For information concerning southern Aroostook County and immediate Houlton area.

Fort Kent Chamber of Commerce
Main St.
Box 135
Fort Kent, ME 04743
Telephone (207) 834-5354

For information concerning northern Aroostook County and immediate Fort Kent area.

Ellsworth Chamber of Commerce
Box 267
Ellsworth, ME 04605
Telephone (207) 667-5584

For information concerning Ellsworth and other points in Hancock County.

Machias Chamber of Commerce
Box 146
Machias, ME 04654
Telephone (207) 853-2917

For information concerning Machias and other areas in Washington County.

Waterville Chamber of Commerce
Castonguay Square
Box 142
Waterville, ME 04901
Telephone (207) 873-3315 or 873-3316

For information concerning some parts of the Belegrade Lakes region.

STATE DEPARTMENTS

The following is a list of state departments where information helpful to the fly fisherman and outdoor recreationist may be obtained.

Maine Department of Inland Fisheries and Wildlife
Information and Education Division
284 State Street
Station # 41
Augusta, ME 04333
Telephone (207) 289-2871

For information regarding fishing licenses and existing regulations, and much other information on Maine lakes, and ponds and fish.

Maine Forest Service
State Office Bldg.
Station #22
Augusta, ME 04333

For information concerning the several hundred primitive campsites located in the unorganized townships of northern Maine.

Maine Publicity Bureau
78 Gateway Circle
Portland, ME 04102

Offers information concerning all aspects of Maine recreation, including fishing, camping, and hiking.

Maine Department of Conservation
Bureau of Parks and Recreation
State Office Bldg.
Augusta, ME 04333

Supplies information on all of Maine's state parks. Information on the Allagash and St. John rivers.

Baxter State Park Authority
Reservation Clerk
P.O. Box 540
Millinocket, ME 04462
Telephone (207) 723-5140

Offers information on Baxter State Park—reservations and maps.

Maine Atlantic Salmon Commission
34 Idaho Ave.
Bangor, ME 04401
Telephone (207) 947-8627

For additional information on the Atlantic salmon in Maine.

PAPER COMPANIES

The addresses which follow are those of pulp and paper companies of their representatives, which offer helpful information and maps for fishermen, campers, and sportsmen traveling on their lands.

The North Maine Woods
Sheridan Road, P. O. Box 382
Ashland, ME 04732
Telephone (207) 435-6213

Represents 14 major landowners in northern Maine; controls in access of 2.5 million acres. Maintains roads and a selected number of primitive campsites on some excellent trout and salmon waters. Fee and permits required. Contact well in advance of visit.

Georgia-Pacific Corp.
Public Relations Dept.
Woodland, ME 04694
Telephone (207) 427-3311

Supplies a sportsman's map of its timberlands in Wahsington County.

Scott Paper Company.
S. D. Warren Div.
Public Relations Office
Westbrook, ME 04092

Supplies a sportsman's map of its timberlands in Maine.

Paper Industry Information Office
133 State St.
Augusta, ME 04330
Telephone (207) 622-3166

Will supply information concerning travel and camping on privately owned timberlands in Maine.

MAPS

U. S. Geological Survey
1200 South Eads St.
Arlington, ME 22202

A condensed compilation of maps in one publication. Excellent and easily carried by fishermen, campers, and canoers.

Topographical maps of Maine.

The Maine Atlas
P. O. Box 81
Yarmouth, ME 04096

Offers detailed county maps published by Prentis and Carlisle Co., Inc of Bangor, Maine. Excellent for fishermen.

The Maine Sportsman
Box 507
Yarmouth, ME 04096

CLUBS AND MAGAZINES OF INTEREST

TROUT UNLIMITED

Nationwide, Trout Unlimited is a major voice in the protection of our trout and salmon resources. As the largest cold water fisheries conservation organization in North America, TU is dedicated to the cleansing of our waterways, the maintaining of appreciable trout and salmon resources for future generations, and protection of habitat. With more than 250 local chapters throughout the United States and Canada, Trout Unlimited has played an important role in preserving our threatened fisheries, and will continue to do so as more and more dedicated trout and salmon enthusiasts join the ranks.

In 1979, there were six local chapters of Trout Unlimited in Maine. The names and addresses of those chapters are included here with the hopes that those who now enjoy Maine's trout and salmon fisheries will take an active part in assuring thriving populations for future years. Much of the enjoyment in fly fishing is preserving—and Trout Unlimited is a good place to start.

Individual membership, $15.00 annually, including a one-year subscription to TROUT, the official publication of Trout Unlimited.

Aroostook Chapter Trout
Unlimited #318
15 Wilson St.
Presque Isle, ME 04769
Telephone (207) 764-1305

Carrie Stevens
Chapter Trout Unlimited #330
P. O. Box 672
Farmington, ME 04938
Telephone (207) 778-3636

Ducktrap Chapter Trout Unlimited #300
5 Lawrence Ave.
Thomaston, ME 04861
Telephone (207) 354-6542

Merrymeeting Bay Chapter Trout
Unlimited #329
RFD #3
Freeport, ME 04032
Telephone (207) 865-4761

Sebago Lake Chapter Trout
Unlimited #328
70 Oceanview Rd.
Cape Elizabeth, ME 04107
Telephone (207) 779-7543

Stream Chapter Trout Unlimited #165
Sunkhaze
P. O. Box 92
Bangor, ME 04401
Telephone (207) 989-2538

National headquarters:

Trout Unlimited
P. O. Box 1944
Washington, D.C. 20013

In Canada:

Trout Unlimited of Canada
2180 Yonge Street, Suite 1704
Toronto, Ontario, Canada M4S 2E7

SPORTSMAN'S ALLIANCE OF MAINE

In 1976, an organization dedicated to protecting the rights of sportsmen was conceived in Augusta, Maine. Since then, membership has grown to more than 4,000, and for the first time in history, Maine hunters, fishermen, trappers, and sportsmen have a full-time voice working for them to help preserve their privileges as outdoorsmen.

Individual membership, $6.00 annually; $10.00 Family, members receive a publication keeping them in tune with what is going on in Augusta concerning hunting. fishing, trapping, snowmobiling, and other outdoor-oriented legislation.

Sportsman's Alliance of Maine
Box 2783
Augusta, ME 04330
Telephone (207) 622-5503

HIKING CLUBS AND INFORMATION

Appalachian Mountain Club
5 Joy Street
Boston, MA 02108

Offers a number of detailed hiking maps of the Appalachian Trail in Maine. Also available is a complete guide book to hiking trails throughout the state-a must for the hiking fly fisherman!

BASS CLUBS

The number of local black bass clubs in Maine is impressive. Many are active only on a local or county scale. One of the largest and most active, however, is Pine Tree Basscasters, sponsors of a series of bass tournaments on some of Maine's most productive bass waters. Schedules, regulations and more information may be obtained from:

Pine Tree Basscasters

c/o Mr. Jim Stewart   or   c/o Mr. Robert Lehioulliea
Box 59   292 West Street
West Kennebunk, ME 04094   Biddeford, ME 04005
Telephone (207) 985-7547   Telephone (207) 499-2605

MAINE OUTDOOR MAGAZINES

Maine is fortunate to have two of the finest educational and informative magazine publications found anywhere in the country. For complete coverage of bilological data concerning Maine wildlife and fish resources, and "where-to-go" and how-to-do" information, both publications are highly recommended.

THE MAINE SPORTSMAN

The Maine Sportsman is a hunting, fishing, trapping, and outdoor-oriented publication offering "where-to-go, how-to-do" information on all areas of the state. Special departments include, Sebago Lake Report, Downeast Report, Bangor Area Report, York County Report, Grand Lake Stream Report, Western Regional Report, Moosehead/Allagash Report, Mid-Coastal Report, and the Southern Aroostook and Northern Aroostook County Report.

There are also special columns on guns, hunting dogs, canoeing, Maine wildlife, and hiking.

For subscription rates and further information, write to:

> The Maine Sportsman
> Box 407
> Yarmouth, ME 04096

MAINE FISH AND WILDLIFE MAGAZINE

This is the official publication of the Maine Department of Inland Fisheries and Wildlife. Published quarterly, it offers biological information on all Maine wildlife and fish resources, written by state wardens and biologists and other Department personnel.

For current subscription rates and further information, write to:

> Maine Fish and Wildlife
> 284 State Street
> Station # 41
> Augusta, ME 04333

DESIGNED BY, AND WITH MANY THANKS TO
TOM CHAMBERLAIN
COMPOSED BY DUARTE TYPESETTING, LEWISTON, MAINE
TEXT TYPE IS TIMES ROMAN, DISPLAY IS SOUVENIR